DATE DUE

3/22			

Demco, Inc. 38-293

GREAT SOCIETY
The Story of Lyndon Baines Johnson

GREAT SOCIETY
The Story of Lyndon Baines Johnson

Nancy A. Colbert

MORGAN REYNOLDS
Publishers, Inc.

620 South Elm Street, Suite 223
Greensboro, North Carolina   27406
http://www.morganreynolds.com

Biography
Johnson
[Lyndon]
Colbert

$20.95 Program 7/02

GREAT SOCIETY: THE STORY OF LYNDON BAINES JOHNSON

Cover photograph courtesy of the Lyndon Baines Johnson Library

Library of Congress Cataloging-in-Publication Data

Colbert, Nancy A.
    Great Society : the story of Lyndon Baines Johnson / Nancy A. Colbert.
       p. cm.
    Summary: Discusses the personal life and political career of the man who served as
  senator from Texas, vice-president, and thirty-sixth president of the United States.
    Includes bibliographical references and index.
    ISBN 1-883846-84-6 (lib. bdg.)
       1. Johnson, Lyndon B. (Lyndon Baines), 1908-1973--Juvenile literature. 2.
  Presidents--United States--Biography--Juvenile literature. [1. Johnson, Lyndon B.
  (Lyndon Baines), 1908-1973. 2. Presidents.] I. Title.

E847 .C52 2002
973.923'092--dc21
[B]
                                                            2001059627

Contents

Lyndon Baines Johnson, 1969
(Lyndon Baines Johnson Library)

Chapter One

A Senator Is Born

As a young man, Lyndon Baines Johnson's grandfather, Sam Ealy Johnson Sr., rode the Chisholm Trail, driving Texas longhorns to the railheads in Kansas. Sam's cowboy days were long over, though, when on August 27, 1908, he galloped through the Texas Hill Country on his black stallion, his white hair flying behind him as he shouted, "A United States Senator was born this morning!"

The new baby was his first grandson. The baby's Great Aunt Kate took one look at the infant and marvelled, "He has the Bunton strain," referring to his wavy coal-black hair, large nose, very large ears, "magnolia white" skin, and dark brown, almost black, "Bunton eye[s]." Bunton men usually stood over six feet tall and were known for their fierce tempers. The baby's grandmother had been a Bunton.

The baby was the first child of Sam Ealy Johnson Jr. and Rebekah Baines Johnson, and for three months they could not agree on a name for him. His mother wanted to name him after a book hero, but his father thought he should be named for one of his lawyer friends. At last Rebekah said she would not get up to make breakfast until her baby had a name. "Would you call him Linden?" Sam asked, naming one of his friends. Rebekah thought a minute and then said, "Yes, if I can spell it L-Y-N-D-O-N." Sam and Rebekah finally named their son Lyndon Baines Johnson.

Rebekah had been a teacher of elocution—the art of public speaking—and had worked for an Austin newspaper as a stringer reporter. She met the dashing young Texas legislator Sam Johnson when she interviewed him for the newspaper. Sam liked this beautiful girl who knew something about politics. They married and moved to a small, four-room cabin in the Hill Country near the Johnson family farm.

Her new home was a shock to Rebekah, who had come from the city of Austin. The cabin sat in the Pedernales River Valley, where the Great Plains ended and the true West began. There was no running water, indoor plumbing, gas, or electricity. Rebekah, who had no experience in homemaking, had to learn to cook on a wood stove. She washed clothes in a tub with water carried in buckets from the well. The homemade lye soap caused her delicate hands to chafe and burn.

Two daughters, Rebekah and Josepha, quickly followed Lyndon. As much as possible, though, Rebekah centered her life on teaching her son. She gave him alphabet blocks to help him learn his ABCs. By age

Sam Ealy Johnson Jr. (left) and Rebekah Baines Johnson (right) named their first son Lyndon (bottom). *(Lyndon Baines Johnson Library)*

three, he could recite Mother Goose rhymes and Longfellow and Tennyson poems. She read him stories from the Bible, from history, and from mythology. Lyndon began to spell at age four and spelled "grandpa" for his grandfather, Sam Johnson.

Lyndon soon discovered he could get his mother's attention by running away. Usually he just ran down the lane to his Grandfather Sam's house, who told him tales from his life, often with colorful exaggeration. Sometimes Lyndon visited more distant relatives or hid in the fields. He refused to answer when his mother called. She would became frantic, but instead of punishing Lyndon when she found him, she covered him with kisses and hugs.

Lyndon also ran away to the nearby one-room school because he wanted to play with the older boys. After awhile, his mother enrolled Lyndon in the school. He liked being the center of attention, so the teacher held him on her lap while Lyndon read aloud. Lyndon's older cousin, Ava, would give him a ride to school on her donkey, but Lyndon insisted on being in charge of the donkey. His aunt commented, "Whatever they were doing, Lyndon was the head."

It was the fashion then to sometimes dress young sons in dresses and let their baby curls grow long. After seeing his son's long, wavy black hair one day, Sam Johnson reprimanded his wife, saying, "He's a boy." He took a pair of big scissors and cut off the curls. Lyndon often followed his father around, wearing a scaled-down version of Sam's big Stetson. He imitated his father's walk and even his coarse speech, much to his mother's distress.

Politics was in the Johnson family's blood. Lyndon's great-great uncle, John Wheeler Bunton, had come to Texas in 1833 in time to fight for the territory's independence from Mexico. He signed the Texas Declaration of Independence and helped write the constitution for the Lone Star Republic. After Texas joined the Union in 1846, Lyndon's maternal grandfather, Joseph Baines, served as Texas secretary of state and a member of the legislature. Lyndon's own father served six terms in the Texas legislature.

Lyndon's father and grandfather spoke out for the rights of the "common man" as opposed to wealthy people and large corporations. Men would gather in the evening to sit on the Johnson porch and talk about how hard it was for a farmer to make a living or how laborers needed to join together to bargain for better wages and working conditions. Lyndon sat beneath his bedroom window that opened out onto the front porch and listened.

Lyndon told his friends he wanted to grow up to be just like his father, and his passion for the underdog grew with the length of his legs. If he was outside playing a game with friends and he heard men discussing politics, he would quit the game and edge over to the group to hear their talk. One time, local politicians gathered on the Fourth of July for speech-making and dinner at the Johnson's house. The children were sent to the kitchen to eat, but Lyndon hid under the dining room table so he could hear every word. Lyndon's genteel mother, Rebekah, did not care for these gatherings of cigar-smoking, whiskey-drinking men who stayed up most of the night, shouting about politics, playing dominoes, and telling stories.

Rebekah preferred for her eldest son to read books, not eavesdrop on his father's political conversations. She wanted him to take violin lessons, but Lyndon refused. Sometimes when Lyndon did something that displeased his mother, she would not speak to him and act as though he were not there. This punishment was torture for Lyndon.

After the first three children were born, Sam Johnson decided he had had enough of farming and moved his family to Johnson City (named after a cousin who had surveyed the land). It was not much of a town. No one in Johnson City had an inside toilet. There was no electricity or running water. There were no movie houses. Rebekah was the only person in town with a college degree.

By the time they moved to Johnson City, Lyndon's father had experienced success in real estate and cattle dealing. Sam hired a local girl to clean their house, saving Rebekah from difficult chores such as scrubbing the floors. Rebekah used her time to start a literary society, where she taught poetry and elocution. The townspeople had never heard of elocution. She also edited the weekly newspaper. After the Johnson family moved to town, another son, Sam Houston Johnson, and a daughter, Lucia, were born.

When Lyndon was ten, his father decided to run for his old seat in the Texas legislature. Lyndon helped pass out campaign handbills and lick stamps. What Lyndon liked best was to travel with his father from farm to farm in their Model T Ford. Sam leaned on a farmer's fence or porch post and talked about the crops and the local gossip. He laughed and joked. When the time came, the constituents knew who to vote for.

Lyndon's father taught him, "If you can't come into a room and tell right away who is for you and who is against you, you have no business in politics." Sam won his seat and kept it until he resigned in 1924. He often took Lyndon with him to the state capitol to listen to debates. As Lyndon grew, he looked and acted more like his father.

When Lyndon was eleven, his Grandmother Eliza Bunton Johnson died, following his Grandfather Sam, who had died earlier. Sam bought the family farm, incurring a large mortgage. The first two years the cotton crop was abundant and the Johnson's were well off financially. Lyndon's father bought his son a pony to ride to school. Buoyed by his family's success, Lyndon bragged to a classmate, "Someday I'm going to be President of the United States."

The third year the cotton crop failed and Sam Johnson's financial ruin began. Eventually, he was unable pay the mortgage and lost the farm. The family had to move back to Johnson City, where they lived in poverty. Sam's money problems caused him to be sick. Before, he had been able to hold his head up, but he now could not pay his bills. Eventually, he had to give up his seat in the legislature. He began to drink heavily.

Lyndon felt his father's failure deeply. Sam had fought long and hard in the legislature for the people and had never taken any favors from special interest groups. Now he had been brought down by circumstances that seemed to be beyond his control, just as many of the people he had championed had been.

Rebekah could not face their reduced position. The fancy clothes she had bought for her children went unlaundered. No one cleaned the house. Some days they only had a little bread and some old bacon to eat. Relatives brought food for the family, saving them from going hungry. Lyndon, the oldest child, took on many of the chores, but he acted out his anger by doing such things as slurping his food, which made his mother cry because she had tried to teach her children good table manners. Finally, after a year, Sam got a job as a foreman of a road building crew working on a road he had proposed when he was in the legislature.

Lyndon entered high school, acutely conscious of how poor he was. Still, he wanted others to notice him. So unlike any other boys his age, he started slicking back his black hair and wearing a bow tie. His favorite subjects were government and history, in which he earned As and Bs.

Lyndon became known as a "talker" and a big joker. He joined the debate team, and he and a friend won the debating championship of Blanco County. Lyndon enjoyed taking Kittie Clyde Ross, a classmate, on picnics and to ice cream socials. But Kittie's parents, who were very respectable people, thought Sam Johnson's reputation for not paying his bills and for drinking made Lyndon an unsuitable companion for their daughter. They forced her to break off the friendship. Lyndon began acting more boisterously, drinking some, and driving recklessly. In spite of this, he was valedictorian of the graduating class of 1924. Lyndon was fifteen years old.

After graduation he shocked and hurt his parents by deciding not to enroll in college. Instead, he and some friends prepared to travel to California. They repaired a Model T Ford, calling it the "covered wagon." His father strongly disapproved of this plan, so Lyndon waited until his father was not home to leave.

In California, the only jobs Lyndon could find were washing dishes and picking grapes. His mother had a cousin in San Bernardino, who was a lawyer. He gave Lyndon and his friend jobs as clerks in his office. He told Lyndon that if he worked hard and learned about "lawyering," as he called it, he could get a license to be a lawyer in Nevada. Lyndon wanted to be a lawyer, so he worked hard as a clerk and read law books at night.

Soon Lyndon was running the office for his cousin, who was often off having a good time. Lyndon's hopes for a future in law were squelched after he discovered that, unlike his cousin had said, he did need a college diploma to become a lawyer in Nevada—and he had to be twenty-one. He was only seventeen. He went home to Texas, disappointed and broke.

Back in Texas, the only job he could find was working on a road building crew. He swung a pick, shoveled dirt, and spread rock all day. He drank and acted wild after work. His Grandmother Baines voiced the family's concerns when she said, "That boy is going to end up in the penitentiary." One night Lyndon got into a fight at a dance and was arrested. Ashamed, he finally told his mother: "I'm ready to work with my brain. If you'll help me get into college, I'll go."

Chapter Two

Wonder Kid of Politics

Because his high school had only eleven grades and was not accredited, Lyndon was poorly prepared for college. In addition, he had been out of school for three years when he returned to Texas, so he needed to take a six-week preparation course before he could be admitted to college.

With a tuition of forty-five dollars a year, Southwest Texas State Teachers College at San Marcos was the only college Lyndon could afford. As part of the entrance requirements, he wrote a paper on current affairs that impressed the head of the English Department. Math was a bigger obstacle, though, and before the test, his mother had to drill him over and over again on problems. Due to his hard work, Lyndon passed all of his entrance exams.

Once enrolled, Lyndon set about discovering who the important people on campus were, what activities to take part in, and what professors to take classes from.

His days were filled with activity. He often mailed his schoolwork home to his mother so she could correct his writing. Lyndon chose history as his major area of study. In his freshman year, he wrote in the *College Star* newspaper, "What you accomplish in life depends almost completely on what you make yourself do."

There were no dorms at Southwest Texas State, so students lived in private homes or boardinghouses. Another student, Alfred "Boody" Johnson (not a relative), invited Lyndon to share a rent-free apartment above the college president's garage. For their keep, President Cecil Evans expected the boys to do chores. In the two years Lyndon lived there, he and Boody painted the garage three times. To earn money, Lyndon picked up garbage and chopped weeds on the college grounds.

His first semester, Lyndon grew to his full height of six feet three and a half inches tall. Most of the trousers he had brought from home were too short. He was embarrassed to go to class but did not have the money to buy new clothes, and he became discouraged. In one of his weekly letters to his mother, he told her he planned to quit college. His mother wrote to his friend Ben Crider, who was still in California, and asked him to encourage Lyndon to stay in school. Ben sent Lyndon all of the money he had in the bank, eighty-one dollars. "I was rich," Lyndon said. "I paid my debts and my next term's bill."

Every time Lyndon saw President Evans, he ran to greet him and offered to run errands and do other small favors. Gradually, he worked his way into the president's grace and was given a job as a messenger. Lyndon set his desk outside the president's door and worked with such enthusiasm and skill that those who came to see President Evans soon thought of Lyndon as his gatekeeper. He always made sure President Evans knew what a good job he was doing. Lyndon told his roommate, "The way to get ahead in this world, you get close to those that are the heads of things."

President Evans had no son, and he enjoyed talking to Lyndon and hearing about his family and their role in Texas politics. Evans realized that Lyndon knew a lot about Texas politics and used him as an informal political adviser. He even took Lyndon with him to Austin to lobby for school funds.

Lyndon liked to boast both about his Texas ancestors and about how smart he was. Other students soon nicknamed him "Bull," a name that stuck through college. Lyndon became a prize-winning debater, driven by his boundless energy and ambition. He became an honors student and served as editor of the *College Star.*

With his editor's status, Lyndon acquired a press pass to the Democratic Convention of 1928. He had fallen in love with an older student, Carol Davis, and invited her and her father to go with him to the convention. The convention was the most exciting event he had ever been to, but Carol and her father were not impressed. Furthermore, Mr. Davis did not approve of this loud, brash student with no prospects from that "no-account Johnson family" courting his daughter.

By the summer of 1928, Lyndon's money problems

worsened. Even with his job for President Evans, his editorship at *College Star*, and rent-free apartment, he could not make ends meet. He spent more than he made on haircuts, clothes, and social activities. He was in debt to the Blanco State Bank, and his student loan was more than he could pay. He had borrowed from everyone he could. He wanted to look and act powerful, but he had no money. Lyndon became depressed. He was silent for days. At last he decided that he had to drop out of college for a year to earn money.

Lyndon got a job as a seventh- and eighth-grade teacher at Cotulla, Texas, only sixty miles from the Mexican border. The school's students were Mexican Americans, and not many teachers were willing to come to this part of Texas, so Lyndon was also appointed principal. He taught, coached, and administered the school. He even served as janitor at times. He told his students that school was their chance to get ahead in life. He said anyone who studied hard could become president of the United States.

As principal, Lyndon saw that improvements were made at the school. After seeing some of his students dig in the garbage for something to eat for breakfast, he started a school lunch program. The school did not have any bats or balls, so Lyndon insisted the school board provide them. He organized volleyball, baseball, and basketball teams, held spelling bees, and started debating teams. At the end of the year, the school board asked him to stay, but Lyndon wanted to finish college.

The year of teaching helped Johnson mature. He

came back to college determined to graduate as soon as possible. During his year teaching, he had earned about fifteen credits by taking correspondence courses, and now he took as many courses as he could.

Johnson also became involved in campus politics. The Beta Sigma fraternity, made up mostly of athletes, were known as the Black Stars. Lyndon had begged his roommate Boody to help him get in, but the fraternity would not accept him. The athletes, although a small percentage of the student population, ran most of the activities and held all of the student offices. A large part of the school budget for student activities supported sports activities, thanks to the influence of the Black Stars.

Lyndon thought the funds should also be used for things such as the debating team, music, and drama. He organized the non-Black Stars—the town students, the non-athletes, the music students, and others—into a secret group he named the White Stars. To convince his classmates of the White Stars' cause, Lyndon talked to students, one by one. The White Stars soon had enough students to run their own slate of candidates for student government, undermining the hold the Black Stars had on the college. The White Stars elected five of their members to the student council and gained choice campus jobs and funds for their activities. Johnson told a fellow student: "Politics is a science. If you work enough at it, you can be president."

The summer before Lyndon graduated, he made his first real political speech at a picnic. Pat Neff was running for state railroad commissioner, and he had given Lyndon's father a job when he needed it. All of the candidates at the barbecue stood up one by one to make their speeches. But when Pat Neff's name was called to speak, no one answered. Finally, Lyndon jumped up to the bed of the old wagon that served as the speaker's platform. "By God, I'll make the speech for Neff," Lyndon shouted. In an arm-swinging defense of the candidate, he spoke for fifteen minutes, ending with the picnickers' cheers.

Welly Hopkins, an influential lawyer who was running for the state Senate, heard Lyndon give that speech and asked him to help with his campaign. Lyndon squeezed time in between classes to work for Hopkins. He organized rallies and passed out literature printed on the college mimeograph machine. He talked his friends into yelling enthusiastically for the candidate at rallies, and in the end, Hopkins won the election.

Lyndon graduated from college on August 17, 1930. His parents, Sam and Rebekah, were especially proud when President Evans introduced Lyndon as, "a young man who has so abundantly demonstrated his worth that I predict for him great things in the years ahead." But the late summer of 1930 was a bad time to begin a career. After the stock market crash on October 29, 1929, the Great Depression had begun, and six million people were out of work.

Johnson had said he wanted to be a politician, a preacher, or a teacher. But even teaching jobs were hard to get. Luckily, Lyndon's uncle, George Johnson, was chairman of the history department at Sam Houston High School in Houston. When a job opened up in the speech department at Sam Houston High, Lyndon was hired.

Lyndon did a good job of teaching his classes, but his love was coaching the debate teams. Sam Houston High had never won a city debate championship, and Lyndon was determined they would. "Act like you're talking to those folks, look them in the eye," he told his students. After choosing his boys' and girls' teams, they began a rugged practice schedule, taking part in practice debates all over Texas. Lyndon drove the students in his Model A, practicing as they went. Coach Johnson also led them in singing and telling jokes. Soon, the debaters were treated like football heroes at the high school, with pep rallies scheduled before debates. The students loved Coach Johnson, and both teams won the city and then the district championships. The boys went on to take second in the state, losing the Texas championship by only one vote.

The next year Lyndon returned to Sam Houston High, and more and more students tried to get into his speech classes. Lyndon enjoyed teaching. He also took time to go to Austin to lobby for pay raises for teachers.

Meanwhile, the campaign manager for Bill Kittrell, who was running for lieutenant governor, heard about "this wonder kid teaching school in Houston who knew more about politics than anyone else in the area." He asked Lyndon to take charge of running the campaign in the Hill Country counties. He believed Kittrell had no chance in those counties anyway, so it could not hurt to let Lyndon run the campaign there. Everyone was surprised when Kittrell won every county in the Hill Country.

In the fall of 1931, the U.S. representative from the Fourteenth District, which included Lyndon's home in the Hill Country, died. The Democratic candidate, Richard Kleberg, who was the heir to the largest cattle ranch in the world, the King Ranch, with its two thousand square miles of land, won the special election held to fill the seat. His political friends advised the congressman-elect to hire Lyndon as his personal secretary because he knew the people in the Hill Country. Lyndon was surprised when a telephone call came to Sam Houston High from Kleberg. When Kleberg offered him the job, Lyndon accepted. Although he liked teaching and coaching the debate team, the job offered him a chance to work in Washington, D.C. His principal granted him a leave of absence, and five days later, Lyndon left for the nation's capital.

Chapter Three

Congressional Secretary

On December 7, 1931, after a long train ride, Lyndon Johnson walked out of Union Station in Washington, D.C., carrying his cardboard suitcase, and saw the dome of the Capitol of the United States for the first time. It was a sight he would never forget.

Excited as he was to be in Washington, Lyndon had little money. He rented a room with another congressional secretary in the subbasement of the old and shabby Dodge Hotel for twenty dollars a month. The bathroom down the hall was shared by all the other government workers living on the floor.

Lyndon exuberantly greeted everyone he met in the hotel, introducing himself and shaking their hands. The first day he brushed his teeth every ten minutes so he could meet people in the hallway. He visited other people's rooms and listened to their life histories. He shared meals with them at the House dining room and at cheap restaurants. These young men knew what was happening inside the Capitol.

The first day Lyndon arrived at Congressman Kleberg's office in the House Office Building, he opened the door of Room 258 to find heaps of gray mailbags with several months' backlog of unanswered mail. Congressman Kleberg's Fourteenth District was twice as big as most Texas districts, with a half million people to represent. It also was home to the nation's largest army post, Fort Sam Houston. Lyndon knew the people of the Hill Country, but he was unfamiliar with the rest of the district that stretched two hundred miles to the south. Lyndon soon learned that Congressman Kleberg was not interested in politics, or the work of being a congressman, preferring instead to play golf and poker. Most days he never came to his office.

"I felt I was going to be buried," Lyndon said later. He and the secretary who was hired to assist him began opening the mailbags. The letters from the district's constituents contained requests for appointments to West Point and government jobs, help with supplying food or paving roads, and assistance on pension and disability problems. Lyndon did not know how to get anything for the constituents.

Lyndon turned on his charm and did favors for the elderly secretaries working for other congressmen in the House Office Building. Soon they were helping him find answers to his questions. Lyndon worked seven days a week, from early morning until midnight. He wrote letters for Congressman Kleberg and often signed them. When his secretary quit, Lyndon sent for two star debaters from Sam Houston High who had recently graduated, both of them sharing the salary of his previous secretary.

Soon, letters to Congressman Kleberg's office were being answered the same day they arrived. Mail was the most important way of keeping in touch with the people back home. On top of his congressional assistant's job, Lyndon performed the congressman's work as well. He made telephone calls to those in power, contacted federal agencies on others' be-

Congressman Richard Kleberg hired Lyndon as his secretary. *(Lyndon Baines Johnson Library)*

half, listened to complaints and acted on them, and gave out patronage jobs. Lyndon understood what it meant to be poor and out of work, and whenever jobs became available he grabbed as many as possible for his people in Texas. Voters began to notice that Kleberg's office was taking good care of the people it represented—and Lyndon began to be recognized as the one who got things done.

The 1932 election brought the Democrats to power in both houses of Congress as well as in the presidency. Lyndon stood at the East Portico of the Capitol and cheered on the day Franklin Delano Roosevelt was inaugurated president. After listening to Roosevelt, Lyndon became a strong supporter of his New Deal programs. When the all-important votes came up for the Agricultural Adjustment Act and Social Security, two key components of Roosevelt's efforts to get the economy moving again, Lyndon strongly advised Kleberg to vote for the president's programs. He told him he would be betraying the people at home if he neglected to vote for those bills. Kleberg listened and voted "Yea."

Lyndon found a way to return a favor when he dis-covered that Ben Crider, the friend who had loaned him money to stay in school, was out of work. Lyndon got him a job as an appraiser with the Federal Land Bank in Houston. Ben said it was the best job he ever had. More and more, the jobs Lyndon got for people were not only in his own district. Texans from all over the state were turning to Kleberg's secretary for help.

To keep up on the issues facing Congress, Lyndon read three daily Washington papers, two New York news-papers, and the local Texas news. He read the Congres-sional Record, pending bills in Congress, official pub-lications, committee reports, and newsletters. He took a pile of government reading to bed with him at night the way other people might take a good book. An older congressional secretary said of Lyndon, "This skinny boy was as green as anybody could be, but within a few months he knew how to operate in Washington better than some who had been here twenty years."

The "Little Congress" was an organization intended

to give congressional staff members training in parliamentary procedures and public speaking. It was modeled after and run like the House of Representatives, using the same rules of procedure and debate as the senior body. But the Little Congress had deteriorated into a social club patronized by a few old-timers. Lyndon felt this organization could be valuable once again and decided to become speaker of the Little Congress.

Up until then, the officers had been chosen by seniority. As he had organized the White Stars in college, Lyndon now used his persuasive powers to bring in new legislative assistants. Everyone on the congressional payroll was eligible to belong, so he invited clerks, secretaries, and congressional post office personnel. He successfully padded the membership, and at the next election of officers, Lyndon was elected the new speaker of the Little Congress—at age twenty-three, the youngest speaker ever.

Lyndon began holding meetings once a week instead of once a month. The members discussed and voted on the same issues as their bosses in the House of Representatives. Lyndon told newspaper reporters that these mock votes were important because they reflected what the congressmen were thinking. Reporters started to cover the meetings of the Little Congress, and prominent speakers began to address them. Lyndon Johnson's name appeared in newspaper reports. Serving as speaker gave Lyndon a reason to ask important congressmen questions and invite them to speak. And "The Chief [Lyndon], being the way he was, would make them remember him," Gene Latimer, an old friend who was one of his staff, said later.

Lyndon made trips home to Texas at every opportunity. During the summer of 1934, while Lyndon was visiting his father at the Texas Railroad Commission office in Austin, the secretary introduced him to a friend named Claudia Alta Taylor. Everyone called Claudia "Lady Bird" because when she was a baby, her nanny said she was as "pretty as a little lady bird." Claudia did not care much for the name, but Lyndon especially liked it. Lyndon made a breakfast date with Lady Bird for the next morning.

From the moment he met her, Lyndon knew he wanted to marry Lady Bird. Her mother had died when she was only five, and her unmarried Aunt Effie had brought her up. Lady Bird's father, Thomas Jefferson Taylor, began his career as a grocer but went on to become wealthy in cotton ginning, farming, and catfish exporting. Lady Bird attended St. Mary's Episcopal School for Girls and then finished her last two years of college at the University of Texas. She graduated with honors, before returning to the university for another year to receive a degree in journalism. She became a reporter for the *Daily Texan*. She also studied shorthand and typing so she would have a good business background.

Lady Bird hesitated going to breakfast with the overwhelming young Lyndon Johnson, but she had planned to interview an architect in the office right next to the coffee shop, so she met him. After breakfast, the brash, talkative young man took her for a drive in the country.

He told her about his family, his education, his job, how much he made, how much insurance he had, and his ambitions for the future. Then Lyndon asked Lady Bird to marry him.

Lady Bird thought it was a joke. Here they were on their first date, and he had asked her to marry him. But Lyndon was serious. She was unsure if she even liked him, but she knew she had never met anyone like Lyndon. She thought he might be after her money, yet she still hoped he was sincerely attracted to her.

Lyndon's visit to Texas was short, so he tried to see Lady Bird as much as possible. He took her out to the Kleberg's luxurious King Ranch and to meet his parents. Lady Bird's father liked the striving young man. He said to his daughter: "You've been bringing home a lot of boys. This time, you've brought home a man."

When Lyndon went back to Washington, he wrote to Lady Bird everyday and telephoned her almost as often. Six weeks after he met her, he drove back to Texas. "Let's get married. Not next year, but about two weeks from now, or right away." Lady Bird had missed him while he was gone, but she still thought he was moving too fast. Her Aunt Effie advised her that if he really loved her, he would wait. But her father snorted at that. "If you wait until Aunt Effie is ready, you will never marry anyone," he said.

Lady Bird decided to visit her friend Eugenia in Austin and ask her advice. Lyndon jumped at the chance to drive her there. As soon as they started the trip, Lyndon insisted she marry him immediately. Lady Bird had packed her trousseau in her suitcase, but she still was unsure. Lyndon called a friend in San Antonio and told him to make arrangements for a wedding at St. Mark's Episcopal Church.

By the time they got to the church, Lady Bird still had not actually said yes. Lyndon had forgotten to buy a ring, so the best man ran out and bought one at the Sears Roebuck across the street from the church. Although the reverend was reluctant to marry the young couple without any formal preparation on their part, Lyndon went to work on him, and he finally agreed to perform the ceremony. Lyndon Baines Johnson and Claudia Alta Taylor were married on November 17, 1934. As they left the church, the reverend shook his head and wondered how long the marriage would last.

After a honeymoon in Mexico City, the newlyweds hurried back to Washington, where they lived in the Dodge Hotel before moving to a small, furnished two-room apartment. They slept on a roll-away bed in the living room. Lyndon thought this was plenty of room after the Dodge Hotel, but it was a change for Lady Bird, who had grown up never wanting for anything.

As Lyndon's mother was as a new bride, Lady Bird knew little about cooking or keeping house, but unlike her mother-in-law, she did not despair. She learned how to pay the rent and buy food and everything else on two hundred dollars a month. And she always saved $18.75 to buy a U.S. Savings Bond every month. She bought a cookbook and taught herself to cook. Every day she set out Lyndon's clothes to wear and put his pen, cigarette

After a whirlwind courtship, Lyndon and "Lady Bird" were married on November 24, 1934. *(Lyndon Baines Johnson Library)*

lighter, handkerchief, and money in his pockets. Excited about being in the nation's capital, she found time to explore the city.

One thing that his pretty new wife could do to further Lyndon's career was to entertain. Even though Lady Bird was an inexperienced cook and their apartment was very small, Lyndon invited guests for dinner. Lady Bird made their guests feel at home with her beautiful smile and gracious manners. One person who especially felt at home in the Johnson's tiny apartment was U.S. Representative Sam Rayburn of Texas. For dinner, Lady Bird made black-eyed peas and cornbread the way Sam liked. A bachelor, Rayburn began to join the Johnson's for breakfast, too.

But Lyndon was beginning to feel dissatisfied. He wanted to be more than a congressional secretary, and he soon got his chance.

Because of the Great Depression, nearly five million young people dropped out of school. Families did not have money for books or pencils or even shoes. First Lady Eleanor Roosevelt called the young people the "Lost Generation," and felt something must be done to help them. She convinced her husband to push a bill through Congress, and on June 26, 1935, the National Youth Administration (NYA) was born. The NYA provided vocational training to unemployed youth between the ages of sixteen and twenty-five and also helped keep students in school.

Each of the forty-eight states would have a NYA administrator. At Sam Rayburn's urging, President

Roosevelt appointed twenty-seven-year-old Lyndon to run the program in Texas. When he and Lady Bird packed up to head home for his new job as the youngest NYA director in the country, he told the other secretaries, "When I come back to Washington, I'm coming back as a Congressman."

Lyndon's job with the NYA was to create work projects to employ the young people of his state. "Put them to work; get them in school" became the administration's motto. Johnson hired his childhood friends, including Ben Crider, as his assistants and went to work. Students went back to school after Lyndon provided money for them to have jobs repairing school buildings and swimming pools. Girls restored books, sewed clothing, and served lunches. The students worked on outdoor projects and learned how to repair farm machinery. Going against the racial segregation of the time, Lyndon made sure black students got jobs, too.

Although the programs were separate, all of the black colleges were included in the student aid program. The Mexican students also were put to work. Young Mexican-American and African-American women were given special dental and medical care and taught cooking and sewing skills.

Lyndon came up with the idea of building "roadside parks." He urged farmers to donate small pieces of their land along the Texas highways and organized students to build shelters for people to picnic and rest. This innovative idea was the forerunner of the superhighway rest stops of today. Eleanor Roosevelt heard of all

Lyndon was doing in Texas and came to visit the young administrator.

After long, hard days that usually ran well into the evenings, Lyndon often took his assistants home for dinner. Lady Bird prepared meals for the hungry young people. Lyndon was building up a core of loyal followers and dedicated students who would be forever grateful for the jobs and opportunities he made possible. Lyndon also met many influential leaders in his efforts to get help for his projects. By 1936, more than twenty thousand youths were in the program. When President Roosevelt came to Dallas, Lyndon lined his cheering NYA workers along the president's route.

One day, Lyndon read the headline that the representative from the Tenth Congressional District had died. Congressmen elected in Texas usually stayed in office for life, so Lyndon had worried he would never get a chance to make good his promise of returning to Washington as a congressman. Here was his chance. The Tenth District included Austin and Johnson City.

Lyndon was not alone in his desire to gain the newly opened office—eight other politicians vied for the same opportunity. Even the deceased congressman's widow said she was thinking of running. Because Texas was then a one-party state, the real race took place in the Democratic primary. This often meant there was a runoff, when the two biggest vote-getters faced off in a race. But this would be a "sudden death" election— whoever got the most votes of the eight candidates would win. Lyndon went to work.

Chapter Four

Pothole Congressman

The first problem Lyndon had to tackle was a familiar one: money. He needed at least ten thousand dollars to run for Congress. Lady Bird's mother had left her a small inheritance, held in trust. She called her father and asked him to advance her ten thousand dollars. Mr. Taylor thought a smaller sum would do, but Lady Bird insisted, and her father sent the money.

President Roosevelt's New Deal programs had made him very popular, so Johnson developed a simple and effective campaign slogan: "A Vote for Johnson Is a Vote for Roosevelt's Program." But Lyndon's main strength as a candidate was his energy and willingness to do what it took to win.

The countryside of the Tenth District covered almost eight thousand miles, an area larger than Delaware and Connecticut combined. Even the radio could not reach all of the widely scattered voters because only one out of every 119 homes had electricity. Lyndon would have to go to the voters.

During the forty-day campaign, Lyndon visited every city and town in the Tenth District. As his father had done, Lyndon traveled the dusty roads, turning off onto paths that crisscrossed fields to visit farmers. Many men remembered Lyndon's father and what a good job "Mr. Sam" had done in the state legislature, so they listened to him. They liked this gaunt, tall young man with a smiling face and huge ears. Lyndon always asked about people's personal lives, saying, "How's your boy?" or "Remember the time . . .?" He recalled names and places. He hugged and kissed the women on the cheek and gave the men a good, solid handshake. Sometimes his assistants had difficulty getting Lyndon out of town after he had given a speech in time to make the next appointment.

Lyndon also talked to African- and Mexican-American voters. He told them a vote for him would mean help for them. They believed Lyndon because he had helped their young people get jobs through the NYA.

Lady Bird licked envelopes and called voters. While the other contestants would rest after giving an important speech, Lyndon finished his speeches and then drove off to talk personally to people all across the district. Of Lyndon's work habits, his friend Gene Latimer, who was assisting on the campaign, said, "We felt he had a chance because we knew he would work harder than anyone else."

Then, suddenly, while giving a speech two days before the election, Lyndon doubled over in pain. He stood up, apologized to his audience, and finished the speech, but he could barely stand to shake hands afterward. "I'm sick," he told his assistant. His friends rushed him to the hospital, where he found out his appendix had ruptured.

From a hospital bed, Lyndon followed the vote counts as they came in. At first, he trailed the leader by about 2,400 votes. But after all the votes were counted, Lyndon had won by more than three thousand votes.

About a month after the election, President Roosevelt was returning from a fishing vacation when he docked at Galveston, Texas. He told the Texas governor to bring the newly-elected congressman to meet him. Aware that President Roosevelt had served as assistant secretary of the navy, Lyndon shared with the president his concern over American naval power. Roosevelt was looking for someone who would vote for a strong navy. When Lyndon Baines Johnson officially became a member of Congress on May 13, 1937, he was appointed to the Naval Affairs Committee, thanks to Roosevelt.

Before he left for Washington, Sam Johnson told his son: "Measure each vote you cast. Is this vote in the benefit of the people? What does this do for human beings?" Lyndon vowed to follow not only his father's words but also his example.

In July, only a few weeks after he had left for Washington, Lyndon's father had a second major heart attack. The doctors said Sam would never recover. Lyndon came to see him and took his dad home from the hospital. On October 23, 1937, sixty-year-old Sam Ealy Johnson Jr. died from heart disease. The family buried him on the small piece of original Johnson Ranch that they still owned.

Sam had died poor. Lyndon set his mother up in a house in Austin and paid off all his father's debts. Although he had been bitterly disappointed by his own political career, Lyndon's father had endowed his son with virtue to stand up for the underdog.

At twenty-eight, Johnson was the youngest congressman in Washington. He launched his congressional career with the same vigor and hard work he had shown in earlier endeavors. He built relationships with the most important people in Washington and dedicated himself to serving the people of his district. Johnson later said, "When I thought about the kind of congressman I wanted to be, I promised myself that I'd always be the people's congressman, representing all the people, not just the ones with money and power."

He began work in his new position by answering letters from the people of his district. He worked so hard writing letters that the skin on his hand cracked and bled. He wrapped a small towel around his hand so that he would not bleed on the letters as he wrote.

Childhood friends, college classmates, and friends from Texas became Lyndon's staff, and they learned quickly how hard they were expected to work. Often Lyndon would shout at them. If he ever hurt an employee's feelings, Johnson would give him a big bear hug. In spite of the long hours and heavy work loads, his staff was dedicated and loyal.

Lady Bird worked for him, too, keeping a scrapbook

President Roosevelt (left) appointed Representative Lyndon Johnson (right) to the Naval Affairs Committee. Texas Governor Jimmy Allred stands between them. *(Lyndon Baines Johnson Library)*

of newspaper articles and pictures of her husband. They bought a movie camera so Lady Bird could take movies of Lyndon to use in his campaigns.

Johnson became interested in the U.S. Housing Authority, a new program that had built low-cost housing to replace the slums in Washington, D.C. His district needed housing help—he still remembered how his Mexican-American students had lived when he was a teacher. He fought to have money appropriated to set up a Housing Authority to build apartments in Austin.

Providing electricity to rural Texas was one of Johnson's main goals. By 1937, Johnson's first year in

Congress, most Americans took electricity for granted. Homes and streets were lighted, and electricity powered factories, trains, subways, elevators, movies, and radios. But people who lived on farms in much of Texas did not yet have electricity. In the less-populated areas of the South and West, it was unprofitable for utility companies to build the necessary infrastructure to bring electricity to rural homes. Johnson promised the farmers he would get electricity for them.

Dams to generate hydroelectric power were necessary if rural Texas was ever going to have its own grid. He worked to pass legislation for a dam project on the Lower Colorado River. Roosevelt had created the Rural Electrification Administration (REA) to help finance the building of electrical lines. But the Tenth District did not have enough people to meet the minimum population necessary to qualify for help. Johnson first petitioned the REA administrator to include his district, before going to the top, writing President Roosevelt with his plea. Roosevelt told the REA administrator to make an exception to the population rule and approve the loan that Johnson requested. Soon the lights went on in the Tenth District. People were so happy, and the young congressman became so popular, that many Texans named their newborn children after Lyndon.

During his early career, Johnson was known as a good "pothole congressman"—a congressman who worked hard to meet the needs in his own district. When the election for Congress came up on November 8, 1938, Johnson ran unopposed and went back to Washington to serve his first full, two-year term as a member of the House of Representatives.

Although he was from the South, Lyndon was exceptional in some ways to the other representatives and senators from below the Mason-Dixon line. The legal standard for race relations in the country had been established by the Supreme Court in 1896 as "separate but equal," however, the "equal" half of this standard was usually ignored. Separation became the rule, resulting in a series of unfair laws that created a societal structure called "Jim Crow." White politicians from the South (although African Americans were also elected during these years) gave little thought to the needs of the black citizens in their districts and states. Johnson worked to see that the African Americans of his district received their fair and equal share of government loans. "He was the first man in Congress from the South ever to go to bat for the Negro farmer," said the assistant administrator of the Farm Security Administration.

Johnson quickly earned the reputation as the hardest working man in Washington. He was so demanding of himself and others that it was not uncommon for his assistants to quit within two months of being hired, despite the scarcity of jobs during these years. It was said that three months working with Johnson was like a decade working with most politicians.

Even though it was hard for Johnson to find time to socialize, he liked entertaining. Part of his job was to build connections with as many people as possible. He could be a very charming host and guest. He had a

Texas-sized presence and enjoyed kidding around and telling jokes. His friends said there was never a dull moment when Johnson was present. He was also always ready to listen to others' problems and complaints, and he trained himself to focus all his attention on the person speaking. He wanted the speaker to feel that he or she was being heard. Lady Bird helped her husband entertain by hosting potluck dinners, backyard picnics, and Sunday afternoon cocktail parties. Some of the people the Johnsons met in these first years in Washington remained their friends for life.

In the House of Representatives, power was based on seniority. Johnson knew how to work hard and get what he wanted for his district, but he also knew how to keep quiet and listen. This helped him earn the respect of senior leaders, particularly Sam Rayburn, who was the Speaker of the House. All this work and skill paid off for his constituents. By 1940, Johnson had wrangled seventy million dollars in federal projects for his district. He would have no trouble being reelected.

Johnson's ambition would not let him rest. He did not want to spend his life in the House. He wanted to go all the way to the top, or at least to the highest level in government he could attain. He decided to try running for a state-wide office in Texas: the U.S. Senate, or maybe even governor. The problem was that in Texas, as in much of the Democratic South, there was not much turnover in politics. Once elected to office, most politicians, if they kept the Democratic Party leaders happy, had no trouble being reelected. It was also unwise for a member of the Democratic Party to challenge a fellow Democratic incumbent. It would ruin a career.

This stability not only meant that southern politicians had secure jobs, it also meant that many of the committees in Congress were chaired by southerners, because they gained more seniority than members from other parts of the country. However, it left few avenues for advancement for more ambitious young politicians—such as Lyndon.

Although Johnson quickly gained a reputation for being a hardworking congressman, he grew anxious to move up the political ladder. *(Lyndon Baines Johnson Library)*

Throughout his life, Johnson became depressed when his ambition was thwarted by conditions beyond his control. He sulked and complained to Lady Bird and close friends, such as Rayburn, about his frustration. He kept on working, though, always looking to prepare himself for the future. He began to make speeches all over Texas and extended his web of contacts. Then, suddenly, another death opened up an opportunity. Texas Senator Morris Sheppard died on April 9, 1941. The next day Johnson announced he was running for his Senate seat.

Lyndon had to run his campaign over the entire state. This put an enormous pressure on him physically, emotionally, and financially. As in his campaigns for the House of Representatives, Johnson worked harder, met more people, and gave more speeches than any other candidate. He even hired an airplane, which was highly unusual in those days, to better travel around the state.

Johnson had a formidable opponent in the Democratic Primary. The governor of Texas, the highly popular "Pappy" O'Daniel, wanted the Senate seat, too. O'Daniel was one of the most colorful men in American politics. Before being elected governor three years before, he had spent ten years as a radio announcer. This was in an era when radio was still novel. He had first appeared on radio to sell flour for the Light Crust Flour Company, when a country band asked Light Crust to sponsor their radio show. Soon O'Daniel went from announcing the show to joining the band in songs, and from there to writing songs and giving talks and lectures. He became famous as a radio personality and the state's best known advocate of traditional, conservative ideas.

When O'Daniel entered the race for governor in 1938, the more sophisticated journalists and politicians in Texas did not think he had a chance. But his message was simple, and one heard frequently in American politics, "Throw the bums out." Much as former television wrestler Jesse Ventura was able to do in Minnesota in 1998, O'Daniel shocked the establishment by winning his first political race.

Johnson knew that Pappy O'Daniel was a formidable opponent. He imitated the governor's style by adding country bands and other festivities to his campaign rallies. He worked harder than ever. He promised localities that he would make sure they got new schools and firehouses if he were elected. He campaigned so hard that he was forced to take several days off to recover from nervous exhaustion. He called upon his contacts among the wealthy businessmen in the state, raised more money than any other candidate, and spent it on campaign workers and rallies. It was even rumored that some of the money was spent to buy votes in the poorer areas of the state.

On election night, the first returns indicated a Johnson victory. "JOHNSON WITH 5152 LEAD, APPEARS ELECTED," read one headline in the *Houston Post*. Then the "late" votes began coming in, and last-minute recounts put O'Daniel ahead. Johnson lost by 1,311 votes. Most of the "late votes" came from strong O'Daniel counties in east Texas, and it was clear that they had been manufactured to make up the difference. In later years, it was revealed that a group of businessmen in the alcoholic beverages industry had conspired to help O'Daniel win the election. They hoped to get him out of Texas because O'Daniel had recently begun proposing a statewide alcohol prohibition. They thought he would do less damage in Washington.

Johnson later admitted that he had made a mistake by announcing his totals first, which let the O'Daniel supporters know exactly how many votes they needed to "find" to put their man over the top. It was a mistake he vowed to never make again. The loss devastated Johnson. "I felt terribly rejected," he said later, "and I began to think about leaving politics." Johnson returned to his seat in the House.

From Washington, Johnson and his colleagues watched with rising apprehension as Nazi Germany defeated country after country in Europe. The British army barely escaped at Dunkirk. Roosevelt believed America should intervene in the war, but the isolationists who controlled Congress, and most public opinion, rejected this idea. Johnson, who had never been across the ocean, agreed with Roosevelt. He thought the United States must resist aggressors or pay the consequences later. The democratic countries had to meet force with force. "The one thing a bully understands is force and the one thing he fears is courage," he said.

In August, Johnson gave his first major speech in the House. He spoke in support of extending the military draft. He felt strongly that the United States should build up its army and navy. In this political endeavor, he used a technique to convince others of his view that he learned from his father and from Speaker Sam Rayburn. "Buttonholing" involved standing toe to toe with a colleague, with one hand draped across the person's shoulder, the other grasping the recipient's coat lapels. Lyndon would look the other representative in the eye, sometimes wagging a finger, and then begin pleading, cajoling and flattering to win the vote. Johnson became a master at "buttonholing," and his legendary perfor-

Lyndon Johnson became the first congressman to enlist for military service after the attack on Pearl Harbor. *(Lyndon Baines Johnson Library)*

mances were soon dubbed "The Treatment." In the debate over extending the draft, it worked. The bill won by one vote: 203 to 202.

On December 7, 1941, only four months after Congress voted to extend the draft, the Japanese bombed Pearl Harbor. The United States declared war the next day. Johnson voted for war and then requested he be put on active duty in the navy. He gave up his ten thousand dollar-a-year salary as a congressman for the three thousand dollar-a-year salary of a second lieutenant, leaving Lady Bird in charge of his congressional office. Johnson described his role in the navy as a "low-ranking set of eyes and ears" for President Roosevelt.

He was assigned to partake in an aerial combat mission over Japanese positions in New Guinea. Facing daily attacks from Japanese fighters, these missions were so dangerous that a tail gunner called them "suicide." Once, Johnson was assigned to a B-26 Marauder medium bomber called the *Wabash Cannonball,* but at the last minute he had to go to the bathroom and another man took his place. Japanese aircraft attacked the *Wabash Cannonball* and it crashed into the Pacific. All on board were killed.

When Johnson joined the crew of the *Heckling Hare,* eight Zeros attacked the flight. Bullets zinged around inside the plane and cannon shells hit the fuselage and wings. Somehow the plane managed to make it back to base. After the ordeal, the tail gunner reported that Johnson remained "cool as ice."

While her husband was on duty, Lady Bird filed his

application to run again for his House seat. Johnson remained on active duty until July 1942, when President Roosevelt ordered all senators and representatives to return to their jobs on Capitol Hill. General Douglas MacArthur, commander in the Pacific theater, awarded Johnson the Silver Star with a battle ribbon for his bravery in the Australian area.

Johnson returned to Washington and the House of Representatives, where he advocated increased education spending because he believed education improved people's lives. He also supported bills to make health care available to all.

While Lady Bird worked for her congressman husband, she longed for a family. She had three miscarriages and was beginning to despair of ever having children. She wanted to use her talent and energy elsewhere. When Austin radio station KTBC went bankrupt and came up for sale, she wanted to buy it. It was a risky move, but they finally decided to take the chance. Radio was thriving, and they knew that if the station made profits, they would finally have enough money to not be dependent on Lyndon's salary. In the first year under Lady Bird's management, the radio station showed a profit.

Then on March 19, 1944, the Johnsons' hope for a family was fulfilled when Lady Bird gave birth to a daughter they named Lynda Bird. Three years later, their second daughter, Luci Baines, completed their family. Often, the small girls had to be cared for "by committee" while their parents worked.

Lyndon and Lady Bird had two daughters, Lynda and Luci.
(Lyndon Baines Johnson Library)

On April 12, 1945, President Roosevelt died suddenly of a stroke, just as the war was ending in Europe. Johnson felt he had lost the most influential friend he ever had. Vice President Harry Truman became president. In August, the new president authorized the dropping of atomic bombs on two Japanese cities. War World II was over.

In the years immediately after the war, Johnson supported the president's foreign policy, including the Truman Doctrine, which pledged U.S. support to any nation fighting against the Soviet Union's efforts to take over their country. The Truman Doctrine was announced to a joint session of Congress on March 12,

1947. It was the official beginning of the so-called Cold War that existed between the U.S. and Soviet Union for over forty years.

Johnson also supported the Marshall Plan, which devoted U.S. money to help rebuild Western Europe. Many in Congress and in America wanted to return to pre-war isolationism and bitterly resented giving taxpayer money to foreign countries. Although the Marshall Plan was not initially popular with his constituents, Johnson was convinced that not helping to rebuild devastated Europe would create conditions that would eventually foster more war. He was joined in the bitter fight to pass the Marshall Plan by a new Republican representative from California named Richard Nixon.

Despite these personal and professional successes, Lyndon still felt that something was missing from his life. He was still feeling the itch for higher office. Pappy O'Daniel had not been happy in Washington and decided not to run for reelection. The problem was, Johnson's congressional seat also was up for election in 1948. If he ran for the Senate this time, win or lose, he would have to give up his seat in the House of Representatives.

Chapter Five

The Guy Must Never Sleep

In 1948, Johnson decided to run for the Senate. While making his announcement, he removed his Stetson hat and flung it into the crowd, declaring, "I throw my hat in the ring."

Johnson knew he was in for another fierce primary campaign. His principal opponent was a deeply conservative Democrat, Coke Stevenson. Since Lyndon's last Senate campaign seven years before, the U.S. had become more conservative. After World War II, most Americans were focused on security and making a better life for themselves and their families. Stevenson, who had served as a popular governor, attacked Johnson for being soft on communism and for supporting the Marshall Plan. These were popular positions in most of Texas, and Johnson knew that he had to find a way to appeal to conservative Texas voters and support the national Democratic Party.

Johnson countered Stevenson by saying he was helping President Truman lead the international resistance of Soviet expansion. He also said that he supported increasing military spending. He made fewer attacks on big corporations than he had made during the 1930s, and promised to support legislation that would limit the power of labor unions. He also downplayed his support for African Americans and other minorities, fearing his concern for them would leave him open to attack from the segregationist Stevenson. Johnson's slogan was "peace, prosperity, and progress," and his primary campaign strength was his youth and experience.

Johnson's claims to being more youthful and vigorous than Stevenson were undercut when bad health interrupted his campaign, just as it had in his first House race and in his loss in 1941. Soon after announcing his plan to run, he began suffering pain in his abdomen. He tried to ignore it, but the pain grew worse. His doctor diagnosed kidney stones and advised surgery. Johnson argued that he could not spare the six weeks it would take to recover from the operation.

Although Johnson had a will of steel, finally he could not go on. The famous woman pilot, Jacqueline Cochran, flew Johnson to the Mayo Clinic in Rochester, Minnesota, in her Lockheed Electra. Doctors used the new cystoscope procedure to remove the stones. Johnson was an irritable patient, and it seemed to the nurses and doctors that his hospital stay would last forever. He ordered three telephones for his room, and one nurse said he made sixty-four telephone calls in one day. After one week, he returned to the campaign trail, desperate to make up for lost time.

Johnson campaigned across Texas in a helicopter called the *Johnson City Windmill.* *(Lyndon Baines Johnson Library)*

He traveled across Texas in a "newfangled" helicopter nicknamed the *Johnson City Windmill,* with the words, "Lyndon Johnson for U.S. Senator" painted on the sides. Each time he dropped into a town or along railroad tracks to shake hands and talk to people, his arrival generated intense excitement. Most people had never seen a helicopter, let alone a candidate for the U.S. Senate. Johnson made as many as thirty stops a day, sleeping only three hours a night.

After the primary vote on July 24, one candidate was eliminated, and Johnson and Stevenson remained. But it did not look good for Johnson. Stevenson led by forty percent of the vote to Lyndon's thirty-four percent—

and the eliminated candidate endorsed Stevenson. It looked like Johnson's hopes would be dashed.

With typical Johnson style, Lyndon refused to give up. After a few days in Washington, Lyndon returned to Texas to work even harder. By the end of the race, he was so exhausted that his secretaries had to hold him up while he shook hands at rallies. Lady Bird worked equally hard. After a serious car wreck on the way to a meeting, she simply asked her hostess if she could borrow a change of clothes before speaking to the group.

The run-off balloting took place on August 6, 1948, but the election was not decided for several days. It was the closest race in Texas history. Unlike 1941, Johnson made sure he had campaign workers at every polling place. He also held out votes from his strongest counties. Stevenson did the same.

Slowly, over the next days, the votes trickled in and the lead changed hands several times. As tension grew, each side accused the other of "stuffing" the ballot boxes. The final tally declared Johnson the winner. Late votes, however, from a southern county with a large Mexican population caused Stevenson to be suspicious, and he demanded an investigation. After a series of court trials and bitter charges of vote stealing, Lyndon was declared the official winner. The winning margin was eighty-seven votes. From then on, Johnson's nickname in Texas politics was "Landslide Lyndon."

Investigations made as late as 1977 indicate that Johnson's supporters did "manufacture" votes to put

Johnson defeated Coke Stevenson (center, with cigar) in a close senatorial election. *(Lyndon Baines Johnson Library)*

their candidate over the top. But they also show just as strongly that Stevenson's campaign also stole votes. The sad truth is that electoral corruption had affected most of the Democratic primaries during this era.

In the November general election against a nominal Republican candidate, Johnson won by more than two to one. Lyndon's grandfather had written in a family album that Lyndon would "be a United States Senator before he was forty." He had almost made it—he had turned forty the previous August.

Now Lyndon was one of two Texas senators. Instead of being one in a sea of 435 representatives, he could practice his powers of persuasion as one of ninety-six senators. He felt comfortable working in the smaller environment, where his buttonholing and other negotiating skills could be more effective.

As usual, he set out to discover the most important people to know, following his own set of rules: "Remember names; Be an old-shoe kind of individual; Be relaxed, easy-going; Don't be egotistical; Be interesting; Get rid of the 'scratchy' parts of your personality; Heal misunderstandings; Practice liking people; Never miss a chance to say a word of congratulations or express sympathy; Give spiritual strength and genuine affection to others."

Lyndon's strong staff, headed by young John Connally, worked from morning until late at night. Eventually, Lyndon arranged for them to be available around the clock. The staff often answered five hundred telephone calls and wrote over a hundred letters each day. Johnson had an amazing ability to remember facts and could reel off names, statistics, and other pertinent information on a wide array of topics. On Sundays, his staff gathered at the Johnsons' home to eat, talk, and enjoy their "Johnson togetherness."

Johnson's hard work earned him the respect of the older senators. He supported the same things he had been fighting for in the House since the war, and this widened perspective regarding the world indicated he was no longer merely a pothole congressman. He did not want to be labeled as a regional politician either, as merely another segregationist southerner. In his first speech on the Senate floor, he stated, "No prejudice is so dangerous as the unreasoning prejudice against men because of their birth, the color of their skin, or their ancestral background." He spoke out against lynching and the poll taxes that were designed to keep blacks from voting. These were strange and courageous words for a senator from the former Confederate state of Texas.

But Johnson was careful to not completely antagonize the southern Democrats, who often chaired the most powerful committees. For example, he voted to keep the Senate rule that allowed filibusters (the right of unlimited debate), calling it an issue of free speech. African-American leaders were frustrated by his justification for the vote. They were bitterly aware that filibusters were often used by segregationists, such as Senators Russell Long of Louisiana and Richard Russell of Georgia, to "talk to death" civil rights and voting rights bills. Johnson voted against all the civil rights legislation that was proposed by President Truman with the claim the laws infringed on state's rights. He was also careful to keep the support of the powerful Texas oilmen by pushing for tax breaks.

During his first two years in the Senate, Johnson needed to build more support among Texas voters. Because of his narrow, controversial victory, his reelection would be uncertain in 1954. His main concern was that he not be perceived as too liberal for Texas. He had closely identified himself with Roosevelt early in his career, and during the conservative 1950s, this left him open to attack as being a socialist who wanted to end the free market system. He worked to change this image by voting to curtail the power of labor unions and by being an advocate of a strong military to counter the spread of communism.

When the Communist North Koreans, supported by the Soviet Union and the newly formed People's Republic of China, invaded U.S.-supported South Korea in 1950, President Truman called on the United Nations to turn back the invasion. Johnson, who thought that the failure of Britain and France to stand up to Hitler had led to World War II, supported the president's decision to send United States troops to help South Korea. He was appointed chairman of the Senate Preparedness Investigating Subcommittee. This was a powerful office for such a new senator. *Newsweek* put him on the cover of the magazine, calling him the "watchdog in chief."

The Democrats suffered heavy losses in the 1950 election, including the Democratic whip. No senator was particularly interested in the job of majority whip, because they were afraid it would identify them too closely to the party. Johnson agreed to take the job. He was expected to keep in touch with all of the senators and know where they were going to be when a vote might come. After having been in the Senate only two years, he became the number two man in the Senate and the youngest whip ever.

Meanwhile, Lady Bird continued to turn the radio station into a more profitable business. In 1951, the Johnsons bought 245 acres on the Pedernales River near where Lyndon had been born. They soon transformed the ranch into a successful working operation and a place where Johnson could go to renew his spirits. Eventually, he even built a landing strip so airplanes could land, which made it easier for him to return home and to bring visitors to the ranch.

When General Dwight D. Eisenhower, who had commanded the Allied armies in Europe during World War II, was elected president in 1952 by a landslide, the Republicans also won both the House of Representatives and the Senate. One of the Democratic senators who lost his bid for reelection was the minority leader. Even though this was not a formal office in the Senate, the minority leader was the most visible Democrat in the country and was chairman of the steering committee that gave out the committee assignments.

Johnson wanted the job. He called senators on election night to ask for their vote. After congratulating John F. Kennedy from Massachusetts on his election, Johnson commented that he thought Kennedy looked like a "nice kid." Of Johnson, Kennedy said, "That guy must never sleep." When the Democrats met to choose their leader in the Senate, Johnson won the vote for minority leader.

Johnson believed that information was power. If he had the most detailed understanding of the way things worked and what his colleagues wanted, he would be successful as minority leader. He called on his staff to gather information. Every time he met someone in the hall, at lunch, in his office, or in the cloakroom, he asked questions, confided, or asked for help. At holidays, his staff delivered hundreds of gifts of candy and

Dwight D. Eisenhower (right) succeeded Harry S. Truman (left) as U.S. president after the election of 1952. *(Library of Congress)*

flowers to secretaries, janitors, waiters, elevator boys, and security guards. Johnson loved to give gifts because he knew they built good will.

The information Johnson gathered helped him make deals on legislation and sway senators to his views. He remembered that when his father gathered the family around the table to make a decision, he would begin with the words from the prophet Isaiah, "Come now, let us reason together." Johnson would "reason together" with senators one-to-one, proving his points, reviewing his position, and advising what had to be done. Johnson also used his knowledge of other senators to make assignments, in an attempt to give each new senator at least one good committee assignment.

By being well informed, Johnson became a highly effective leader in the Senate, with a network of allies to show for it. Hubert Humphrey, who also came to the Senate in 1948, later remembered: "From the beginning, he understood the most intricate working of the Senate. He knew how to appeal to every single senator and how to win him over." Johnson practiced "consensus politics." At the end of one of his busy days, Johnson would say he would try to "figure out how to do it better tomorrow."

Johnson worked to move the Democrats to a more moderate, middle-of-the-road position on issues. At that time, the party was badly torn between the liberals, who were pro-labor and pro-civil rights; the supporters of President Truman, who wanted tighter controls on labor and wanted to "go slow" on civil rights; and the Dixiecrats, who were very conservative and intensely segregationist. Eisenhower was a very popular Republican president, so Johnson encouraged his fellow Democratic senators to make decisions on legislation based on its merits, not party affiliation. Remembering his father's words, Johnson said: "I have one yardstick that I try to measure things by: Is this in the national interest? Is this what I believe is best for my country?"

Although the Korean War ground to a stalemate in 1953, another problem area in Asia came to the forefront. At the end of World War II, Communist Ho Chi Minh had declared himself head of the Republic of

Vietnam and started a war in 1946 to drive the French out of the region. Ho Chi Minh insisted he was fighting a war to liberate his country from colonial oppression, but many in the West feared communist expansion. Until then, the United States had been giving the French arms and other aid. After Ho Chi Minh came to power, the French asked for direct military help. Johnson said he opposed sending any American military to fight with the

Communist leader Ho Chi Minh drove the French out of South Vietnam. *(Library of Congress)*

French. Secretary of State John Foster Dulles wanted to send airpower and sea power, reasoning that if "one pro-Western Asian nation fell to the Communists, the others would quickly follow." But in May 1954, the French were defeated and agreed to leave Vietnam. A truce negotiated in Geneva, Switzerland, divided the country into North Vietnam, which was under communist control, and South Vietnam, which was under a government supported by the United States. Independence was also granted to Cambodia and Laos. As soon as the French left, tension and fighting began between North and South Vietnam.

The same month in the United States, the Supreme Court focused more attention on civil rights when it ruled in the case of *Brown* v. *Board of Education of Topeka, Kansas* that separate schools for black and white students was unconstitutional. Johnson realized that this was the "most significant Supreme Court decision in a hundred years." He also knew that most of the white voters in Texas expected him to speak out against it on the Senate floor, and he was up for reelection in a few months. But, if he ever wanted to be president, Johnson recognized he would have to win votes in northern states, where response to *Brown* v. *Board* was more popular. After careful consideration, he said that there was little to be gained by attacking the *Brown* decision. It was now the law of the land, and he advocated progress.

Preparing for the 1954 election, Johnson traveled widely in Texas, telling the voters, "Mr. Eisenhower is the only President we've got," and that he planned to work with the Republicans to show the Communists the U.S. was united. He stressed how hard he worked in Washington and visited every major city in his home state. He greeted children from the public schools, the African-American schools, and the parochial schools. He told them to tell their "mothers and daddies to vote for Lyndon Johnson." He knew that his reelection to the Senate would put him in the running for the presidential nomination in 1956. A *Time* magazine article had mentioned his name as a possible candidate.

The Democrats won big in the House and took a two-vote lead in the Senate in 1954. Johnson won by a margin of three to one, and he became the youngest Senate majority leader in history. He continued to work hard and was a highly-effective leader. Humphrey said that he had never known a man who was such a good judge of character.

After becoming the majority leader, Johnson began to suffer severe back pain that continued until his doctor made him go to the Mayo Clinic, where a kidney stone was again discovered. This time, after Johnson went through surgery, he stayed at the hospital for eleven days before spending two weeks at his ranch.

Back in Washington, a fight over the income tax was heating up. Johnson proposed a plan that would benefit mostly low-income families and close many tax loopholes for corporations and wealthy taxpayers. The plan was too liberal for the southern Democrats, and they voted with the Republicans to defeat it. Johnson had lost his first major battle as majority leader, but he had learned his lesson. Johnson's new strategy would be to compromise in order to get some of what he wanted.

As the majority leader, Johnson controlled what came to the Senate floor and could speed up or slow down a vote. "Timing can make or break a bill," he said. If a bill was ready and he had the votes, he signaled the clerk by twirling his finger in a circular motion to start the roll call. If he wanted to delay the vote, he would push his hand down to show the clerk he wanted to slow things down. Johnson would get others to applaud a bill if he favored it and he also let senators know when their attendance on the floor was unwanted. He always counted his votes ahead of time. By mastering the action on the floor, Johnson increased his authority. A *Newsweek* article pointed out how the Senate had passed ninety bills in only four hours and forty-three minutes under Johnson's leadership.

After his kidney stone operation, he did not give his body a chance to fully recuperate before returning to work. By the end of June 1955, he weighed more than he ever had in his life and was smoking three packs of cigarettes a day. On Friday, July 1, 1955, Johnson ate dinner with his friend Speaker of the House Sam Rayburn, who thought he looked very tired. He told Johnson to get some rest.

The next day on a trip to visit friends for the Independence Day holiday, Johnson thought he was suffering from acute indigestion and asked for a Coke. Then pain shot up his left arm and his chest felt "as though there were two hundred pounds on it." An ambulance rushed him to Bethesda Naval Hospital. He had suffered a heart attack. He jokingly told Lady Bird to have his tailor finish the blue suit he had recently ordered because he would need it "no matter what."

While he was in the hospital recovering, Johnson wanted his wife to be with him at all times. Lady Bird stayed there six weeks. Because most men in the Johnson family had died of heart disease at a relatively early age, he was convinced his time was running out.

Johnson was again a difficult patient. Even though his doctor wanted him to remain calm, he shouted at the newscasters on the radio when he disagreed with their reports. His staff took over the floor doctor's office. He had rounds of visitors, including President Eisenhower and Vice President Nixon. Finally, the doctors ordered him home to the ranch—to rest.

At home, in the quiet of the ranch, Johnson sunk into depression. He hated being dependent on others. He talked about resigning from politics. One day he would rage, and the next day he would be submissive. Lady Bird knew what he needed was love and reassurance. He gave up smoking, swam in the pool, and cut out his favorite fried foods. He slowed his pace and even began to read books for pleasure and listen to music. He finally had time to spend with his growing daughters. They talked and played cards.

His staff kept him up to date on the activities in the Capitol. Johnson even held press conferences at his ranch, which was frequently visited by politicians. In November, he gave a speech outlining his "Program with a Heart." He called for an extended Social Security bill, tax relief for low-income groups, hospital and school building programs, public roads, a farm program, and housing.

By January 2, 1956, the opening day of the second session of the Eighty-fourth Congress, Johnson was back as majority leader with more vigor than ever. At first he tried to obey the doctor and take it easy, but soon he was operating at full steam.

As the Democratic convention of 1956 neared, Johnson became known as a national figure. His old friend John Connally nominated him as a candidate for president, calling him "a man for all sections." Rebekah Johnson came to Chicago as a guest at the convention, glowing with pride for her son. But Lyndon had two points against him at the convention: He was recovering from a major heart attack, and he was a Texan. Adlai Stevenson of Illinois, who had been the candidate in 1952, was chosen again as the Democratic candidate for president. In the end, it did not matter very much. Stevenson lost to President Eisenhower, but Johnson retained his leadership of the Senate.

At the convention, Lady Bird noticed lumps on her mother-in-law's arms. Soon after, Rebekah Johnson was diagnosed with lymph gland cancer. She died on September 12, 1958, at age seventy-eight.

By 1957, the pressure to act on a civil rights bill had grown so intense that Lyndon took leadership of the issue. Although weakened by its opponents, the Civil Rights Act of 1957 was the first civil rights bill enacted in eighty-two years. It created the Civil Rights Commission and installed some voting rights protections.

After Congress adjourned in 1957, the world was surprised when the Soviet Union launched the first man-made satellite, *Sputnik I*. The U.S. prided itself on having the greatest engineers and the most money, but the Russians had won the race, becoming the first nation to gain a foothold in space. Johnson quickly arranged to open hearings on how the U.S. could have fallen behind in the "space race" and how America could catch up. Eisenhower was cool towards Johnson's committee, commenting: "Johnson can have his head in the clouds. I'm going to keep my feet on the ground."

In December, the United States fired its own, smaller satellite, *Vanguard I*, which exploded and fell back to earth. Finally, on January 31, 1958, *Explorer I* successfully made it into orbit. In February, Johnson organized a Senate subcommittee on Aeronautical and Space Science and appointed himself the chairman. The National Aeronautics and Space Administration (NASA) was established and set up headquarters in Houston, Texas, at the Johnson Space Center. President Eisenhower asked Senator Johnson to present a United States resolution to the United Nations calling for peaceful exploration of outer space.

As the presidential election of 1960 drew closer, Eisenhower took a firm stand on balancing the budget. Almost every bill that came to the Senate required federal funding. Johnson wanted to press on with these needed bills, but he knew President Eisenhower would veto them. Two of the few issues before the Senate that were not dependent on federal aid were statehood bills for Hawaii and Alaska.

Statehood for Alaska had the votes, but the southern segregationists opposed statehood for Hawaii because of the racial mix of its population. Johnson brought the Alaska bill to the floor first. When the vote passed, making Alaska the forty-ninth state, people jammed in the Senate gallery cheered.

The Hawaii statehood bill was a different story. Johnson used all of his famous methods, giving his fellow senators The Treatment. He stressed one point to the Republicans, another to the Democrats, crossing the Senate floor over and over again to discuss the issue. When he twirled his fingers to start the roll call, aides darted out to round up the senators. Statehood for Hawaii won by a vote of seventy-six to fifteen.

The Civil Rights Act of 1957 had many shortfalls. It did little to open housing, education, or to protect voting rights. In effect, African Americans were still second-class citizens. On February 1, 1960, black college students sat down to eat at the Woolworth dime store counter in Greensboro, North Carolina. Blacks had always stood to eat at the counter before. After they were refused service, the students politely sat in protest at the lunch counter for two hours. As they left, they recited the Lord's Prayer. The next day, the students returned again. Within two weeks, the non-violent lunch counter sit-ins spread to fifteen cities in five states. Angry whites protested and brawls began.

Johnson said, "The Senate is going to do what is right." He brought a civil rights bill that had been passed by the House to the floor. The southerners responded by beginning a filibuster. Johnson announced round-the-clock sessions and ordered forty cots put up in Senate offices so that enough members would always be ready for a quorum call. If a quorum (the minimum number that must be present) could not occur, the Senate could be adjourned and the bill would die.

Johnson's team of senators spent thirty-seven days and nights at the Senate before a clean-up break was allowed. The filibuster continued for a record 125 hours. At last, Congress passed a civil rights bill, and President Eisenhower signed it into law on May 6, 1960. Again, though, the bill was inadequate. The only real improvement was the right to appoint federal voting referees to register black voters, and it set criminal penalties for bombing and bomb threats against civil rights workers. One senator said, "it was only a pale ghost of our hopes."

By 1960, Johnson had served for twenty-four years in Congress—twelve years as a representative and twelve years as a senator. His health was restored from the heart attack, and he was growing restless for the next challenge.

Chapter Six

Vice President

Johnson had always wanted to be president. In 1958, as Senate majority leader, he had taken the precaution of convincing his supporters in the Texas State Legislature to pass a law that would allow him to run for reelection to the Senate and for national office at the same time. That way, if he failed to make it to the White House, he could still serve in the Senate.

Johnson had reasons not to take the gamble of running for presidential office. His health was always an issue. He also hated the idea of losing. To compound his concerns, Johnson had serious doubts about the probability of a southerner being elected to the presidency. He told one friend that with the Civil War only a hundred years in the past, it was still too early for a man from the old Confederacy to be elected. Although his on-again, off-again support for civil rights had separated him from the typical southern politician, the stigma still remained.

Speaker of the House Sam Rayburn wanted Johnson to run. Senator John F. Kennedy of Massachusetts was emerging as the front runner for the Democratic nomination, but Rayburn—and Johnson—doubted that a Roman Catholic could win. Johnson considered Kennedy to be a playboy—a young "whippersnapper" who "never said a word of importance in the Senate." But he still would not commit himself to run. Rayburn went ahead and formed a "Johnson for President" group with headquarters in Austin.

When he did not stop Rayburn from forming the group, his supporters realized what Johnson's strategy was. He did not want to run in the Democratic primaries, where he would have to campaign in various states. Instead, he wanted to be drafted, to have it look as though the party had turned to him as the best candidate. This plan would only work if no one candidate showed up at the Democratic Convention, to be held in Los Angeles in 1960, without enough votes to win the nomination on the first ballot.

Johnson, however, had underestimated the appeal of John F. Kennedy. Kennedy had not been a formidable senator—he had spent most of his time preparing to run for president. But Kennedy had something Johnson lacked, two traits that were becoming more important as American politics entered the television age: charm and style. Kennedy "looked" like a president. Television was never Johnson's medium. He looked, and sounded, like a lumbering, Texas deal maker.

Johnson, convinced people would side with him because he was a hardworking senator, stuck to his Senate duties while all of the other presidential hopefuls took to the campaign trail. In the meantime, Kennedy won state primaries and charmed voters from California to the hills of West Virginia. As late as June 1960, forty-three percent of journalists considered Johnson to be the strongest candidate. Republican President Eisenhower said that Johnson was best prepared to become president.

Finally, on July 5, Johnson announced he would run, saying: "The next president is not going to be a talking president or a traveling president. He is going to be and should be a *working* president." His campaign strategy was to discredit Kennedy. Johnson called him a young, "scrawny little fellow." Johnson said, "The vice presidency is a good place for a young man who needs experience." When stories of Kennedy's poor health surfaced and Kennedy was forced to reveal his health records, Johnson quipped that Kennedy's pediatrician had said he could run for president.

Johnson's failure to get out and campaign had hurt him, as was made clear in his first minutes in Los Angeles. When he arrived at the airport, crowds of people were waiting to see the presidential-hopefuls arrive. Johnson entered and bowed and waved to the crowd, but no one seemed to know who he was. He had been overshadowed by the photogenic John F. Kennedy. Nevertheless, Sam Rayburn put Johnson's name into the hat for nomination as the party's candidate for president of the United States at the Democratic National

Johnson believed Senator John F. Kennedy (right) lacked enough experience to be an effective president. *(Lyndon Baines Johnson Library)*

Convention, saying, "We must offer a man who has demonstrated that he can lead."

As the roll of the states began, Johnson watched on TV from his hotel room. The states announced their votes alphabetically, and until Illinois voted, Johnson and Kennedy were neck and neck. But Johnson faded as the second half of the states were called. The last state, Wyoming, cast its votes for Kennedy. Johnson had received 409 votes, but John F. Kennedy had won the Democratic nomination on the first ballot. Johnson fought to contain his rage. He was convinced that he was the better candidate; that he had lost a popularity contest to a rich boy from New England. He sent a

Johnson agreed to join John F. Kennedy as his running mate in the 1960 presdential election. *(Lyndon Baines Johnson Library)*

telegram of congratulations to Kennedy and went to bed.

There was still the question of the vice-presidential candidate. Because Kennedy was a Catholic from New England, it was important that his running mate represent the large demographic of voters who were Protestant and not from the Northeast. Kennedy and his brother Robert, who ran the campaign, knew they needed help in the South and the West. As a Texan, the majority leader of the Senate, and the runner up to Kennedy in the nomination, Johnson seemed a good match. Although Robert Kennedy and Johnson deeply disliked one another—it was finally decided to ask Johnson to join Kennedy on the ticket.

Lyndon Johnson was asleep when Kennedy called and asked him to be his running mate. Many of Johnson's friends and colleagues, even Sam Rayburn, did not want him to accept. Many of Kennedy's group were upset that Johnson had been offered the slot. They did not trust Johnson, and most thought he was not liberal enough. But everyone thought it was the strongest possible Democratic ticket. Johnson did not want to be vice president, but he finally said: "I may owe a responsibility to try to carry this country for the Democratic Party." He walked out into the hall of the hotel and climbed up on a chair to announce. "Jack Kennedy has asked me to serve. I accept."

After a few days pause for planning, Johnson threw himself into campaigning—traveling and giving speeches. He had

After agreeing to be John F. Kennedy's running mate, Johnson traveled aboard the *LBJ Special* during the 1960 presidential campaign. *(Lyndon Baines Johnson Library)*

a hard time accepting that the young "whippersnapper" was now his boss. But he had agreed to serve, and serve he would.

He started the campaign in Boston. After only a few women came out to meet him at the airport, he became disappointed. When Johnson reached downtown, he saw a policeman directing traffic from a horse. He got out of the limousine and said, "If you will get off that horse, I'll get on," and he suddenly attracted a crowd. The campaign was on. In the South, Johnson campaigned from a train called the *LBJ Special*.

His campaign manager complained that one problem with Johnson was that every time he saw a group of six people he wanted to make a speech. Usually two or more people wrote Johnson's formal speeches, but he always made changes and often scrapped the drafted speeches altogether. Kennedy was different; he always gave the speech that was written for him. Johnson always spoke longer than he was supposed to. He would say, "Don't let me speak but fifteen minutes," and although Lady Bird would slip him a note to tell him time was up, he always continued to talk. At last she would end up tugging on his coat. As the two-month campaign neared its end, Kennedy felt he had made the right choice. Johnson was often difficult to work with, but he worked extremely hard and he loved the crowds.

Ironically, Johnson ran into the ugliest crowd of the campaign in Dallas, Texas, when a group of right-wing extremists jeered and booed him. They were upset with the Democratic Party's support of racial equality and were convinced that communists controlled the party. The crowd blocked the lobby of Lyndon's hotel. Police came to escort Johnson and Lady Bird through, but he refused. "If the time has come when I can't walk through a lobby of a hotel in Dallas with my lady without a police escort, I want to know it," he said and walked into the crowd. A sign bounced off Lady Bird's head, and a stick almost hit her eye. Television cameras recorded the Johnsons as they made their way through the ugly crowd. Lyndon made sure to walk slowly so there would be plenty of film footage. When the story ran on national news, there was an outpouring of sym-

Lyndon and Lady Bird pushed their way through a crowd of angry protestors in Dallas during the 1960 presidential campaign. *(Lyndon Baines Johnson Library)*

pathy for him and Lady Bird—and the Democratic ticket.

Election day was on November 9, 1960, but it was not until the early morning hours of November 10 that the country knew who had been elected president. John F. Kennedy and Lyndon Baines Johnson were elected in what was, until the Bush-Gore race of 2000, the closest election in U.S. history. Lyndon's home state of Texas had voted for Kennedy-Johnson.

Lyndon was also reelected to his Senate seat, and it was with a heavy heart that he resigned to serve as vice president. He was going from one of the most important and active jobs in politics to a job that an earlier vice president, John Garner Nance, had said was "not worth a bucket of warm spit."

On inauguration day, January 20, 1961, seven inches of snow covered the ground in Washington. The winter sun reflected off the snow and the temperature rose over twenty degrees. Lyndon Johnson was sworn in as the thirty-seventh vice president of the United States by his old friend, Speaker of the House Sam Rayburn. They used the Holy Bible of Lyndon's mother, Rebekah.

The vice president serves at the president's discretion. The job is as large or as small as the president wants it to be. The only official duty is to chair the Senate, where he can only vote if there is a tie.

President Kennedy appointed Johnson chairman of the Space Council that was established to advise him on the nation's space policy. The U.S. was still trying to catch up with the Soviet Union in space and needed to devise a plan. After studying the matter, Johnson gave the president the Space Council's report. The council believed the United States should undertake a project to land a man on the moon. President Kennedy asked Congress to approve spending twenty billion dollars to send a man to the moon by the end of the decade.

But Vice President Johnson felt unimportant and impatient in his position, and President Kennedy grew frustrated with him. "We never got a thing done today," the president said. "Lyndon never stopped talking." Kennedy worked to try to keep Johnson happy. At state dinners, he invited the Johnsons upstairs first. Then together, they would all descend the stairs with a color guard to greet the guests. Sometimes for smaller, more intimate parties, however, the Johnsons' name was left off the guest list entirely. At the last minute, the president would call and invite them. Johnson knew he would never be part of the president's "in-group."

Even though Johnson didn't have much power as vice president, he did have status. He was the second in line in the U.S. government. He tried to put that status to good use by visiting other countries. He had never traveled much before, except to Mexico and briefly to Europe at the end of World War II, and he didn't speak any language but English and a little Spanish and Hill Country German.

Now he visited the people of Asia, Africa, India, and elsewhere. He walked the streets of distant capitals handing out trinkets and shaking hands. The poor people of the world reminded him of the ordinary Texas farmers and small town people he had known all his life.

They usually could not understand his long speeches, but they sensed he cared.

Johnson visited thirty-three countries and traveled 120,000 miles during the less than three years he was vice president. People advised him, "Don't get out among the people because they're dirty," and "don't shake hands unless you wear gloves." Johnson ignored them all. Lady Bird and Lyndon got up early in the morning and went to the market in town squares. He ate raw fish, hugged people—even lepers on one occasion—and kissed babies. Johnson said, "When I looked in the eyes of the mothers, they had the same look as the mothers in Texas." Johnson acted as if he were running for election in the countries he visited. One U.S. ambassador told a translator, "If Lyndon forgets and asks for votes, leave that out." He would always leave the people he visited with the invitation, "Now you-all come to see me in Washington."

His staff was relieved when only one person out of the tens of thousands of people Johnson invited to the United States took him up on his offer, a Pakistani camel driver named Bashir Ahmad. Johnson brought him to the United States and entertained him at his ranch. Bashir Ahmad was a dignified, gentle man, and a devout Muslim. The Americans responded to him warmly.

Johnson's visit to Berlin, Germany, in August 1961, was unlike any other trip he had taken. Berlin was one of the most sensitive places in the world during the Cold War. The city was divided into the Communist east and the capitalist west. Because thousands of East Berliners, usually the ones with the most skills and education, were escaping across the fence that separated them from West Berlin, the East German government had erected the tall, concrete Berlin Wall.

To reach Berlin, a hundred-mile road ran from the west through the Russian Zone of Germany. Premier Nikita Khrushchev of the Soviet Union threatened to close it in order to seize control of West Berlin. President Kennedy planned to send an additional fifteen hundred troops to the city. Johnson was sent to West Berlin to tell the people that President Kennedy was going to keep the American's pledge to fight for their freedom. When the American troops finished the hundred-mile trip to Berlin through the Russian Zone without an incident, Johnson was there to greet them with a huge crowd of cheering West Berliners.

When he returned home from Germany, Johnson's old friend Sam Rayburn met him at the airport. Lyndon could see that Rayburn, who was the longest serving speaker of the House in U.S. history, was dying. A few days later Rayburn went home to Texas and never returned to Washington. He died of cancer.

President Kennedy wanted Johnson to go to Southeast Asia on a fact-finding mission. Johnson did not want to go, but Kennedy sent him with a message to Ngo Dinh Diem, the leader of South Vietnam, that the U.S. president planned to increase U.S. aid by about forty million dollars for water and electricity.

In his travels through South Vietnam, Johnson witnessed how the people suffered. Poverty and corruption were rampant. He believed troops and supplies were needed to win a conventional war against the North Vietnamese army as well as to fight the Viet Cong, Communist fighters who were fighting a guerilla war from within South Vietnam. The people needed food, medicine, and education. Johnson wrote Kennedy a long report stressing the danger posed to the military efforts to stop the Communists. Despite these misgivings, he recommended a program of military action.

After traveling to Vietnam, Johnson told Kennedy he was tired of traveling, but Kennedy sent him to the Middle East. Huge crowds poured out everywhere to greet him. One aide claimed Johnson shook three hundred hands in five minutes. In Iran, they said he could have been elected shah. Even in Turkey, where customarily no one comes out to see foreigners, the Ankara town square was filled wall-to-wall with people. Where there were poor people, Johnson's campaigning habits emerged, always doing his best to impress the crowds with America's goodwill.

Johnson was named chairman of the Presidential Committee on Equal Opportunity, which provided him a way to continue to work on civil rights. He made speeches all over the country on the need for equal opportunities for minorities. President Kennedy sent a civil rights bill to Congress in 1963, but Martin Luther King Jr. criticized it as being inadequate "tokenism."

Even with all of his efforts to remain in the limelight, by 1963, Johnson was practically an invisible man. The

As vice president, Johnson toured countries all over the world, including Vietnam.
(Lyndon Baines Johnson Library)

comedy television show, *Candid Camera*, did a segment of street interviews where they asked people if they knew who Lyndon Johnson was. Not a single person recognized his name.

Anticipating the 1964 elections, Johnson complained that he could not stand six more years of "semi-retirement" as vice president, although he worried that Kennedy would drop him from the Democratic ticket. He knew that Robert Kennedy, now serving as attorney general, wanted his brother to get rid of Johnson. If that happened, his career would be over. It would be almost impossible for him to gain the Democratic nomination in 1968 if Kennedy served two terms.

By the fall of 1963, it was clear that Texas, one of the states with the largest number of electoral votes, was in danger of going Republican. The biggest cause of friction was the national Democratic support for civil rights, which the state's Republicans had come out against. To further aggravate the problem, John Connally, who was now governor, was in a feud with the leader of the more liberal wing of the party.

President Kennedy was reportedly upset that Johnson had not been able to better control his home state, and he decided that he should take a trip personally to Texas. Adlai Stevenson, who had been in Dallas recently for a meeting and had seen anti-Kennedy placards and fliers, advised the president not to make the trip. Johnson, too, thought this was the wrong time to go. But Kennedy insisted. First Lady Jacqueline Kennedy said she wanted to go, too.

The morning of their arrival in Dallas, on November 22, 1963, the *Dallas Daily News* carried a full-page ad paid for by a local group of ultraconservatives that accused President Kennedy of being pro-communist. As the cavalcade drove slowly through the city, shots rang out. Jackie Kennedy screamed, "Oh, my God, they have shot my husband."

At Parkland Hospital, the assistant press secretary approached the stunned Johnson and said, "Mr. President." He then asked how they should announce that President Kennedy was dead.

Chapter Seven

The President's Hand

After hearing that President Kennedy had been assassinated, the country was in a state of shock. People cried and prayed, staring at the unfolding drama on their televisions. Onboard Air Force One, the plane that carried Kennedy's body back to Washington, Lyndon Baines Johnson was sworn in as president, with Jacqueline Kennedy by his side. The plane landed in Washington at twilight, as the moon inched its way up into the sky. A battered, gray hearse drove to the plane to receive the casket. Beautiful Mrs. Kennedy, still wearing her bloodstained clothes, followed. Then the new president and Lady Bird came down the steps.

Against the dark of night, in a glare of floodlights that seemed to drain the color from his face, the new president raised his voice and said: "This is a sad time for all people. I will do my best. I ask for your help—and God's."

President Johnson believed the most important thing

he could do at that time was to reassure the country and the world. He called former Presidents Truman, Eisenhower, and Hoover and asked for their help and advice. He met with congressional leaders. He asked Kennedy's cabinet to continue on in their posts.

During Johnson's first full day in office, he made his first foreign policy decision. He authorized continuation of military aid to Vietnam. On that day, true to his usual pattern, Johnson made thirty-two phone calls and met with eleven people, some two or three times.

On the next day, a Sunday, the new president, his wife, and daughter Luci went to church and afterwards drank coffee with the parishioners in the church hall. As Lyndon was leaving, Secret Service men grabbed him and raced him to the car. Lee Harvey Oswald, the man who had shot Kennedy from the Texas School Depository building, had been shot and killed—live on television—while being transferred to jail. There were fears of a deep conspiracy taking place.

On Monday, the nation mourned as John Kennedy was laid to rest. President Johnson with his wife and daughters, Lynda, who was a sophomore at the University of Texas in Austin, and Luci, who was sixteen and in high school, walked in the procession behind the Kennedy family from St. Matthew's Cathedral to the cemetery. The Secret Service and Federal Bureau of Investigation had tried to talk President Johnson out of walking the route. But Johnson decided he had to walk. President Kennedy was buried in Arlington National Cemetery.

After the assassination of John F. Kennedy on November 22, 1963, Lyndon Baines Johnson swore to uphold the duties of president. Lady Bird is on his left and Jacqueline Kennedy is on his right. *(Lyndon Baines Johnson Library)*

Royalty, chiefs of state, and ministers came from seventy countries to pay their respects. The staff lined the guests up alphabetically by country and made cue cards for the president. At the reception, Johnson formally greeted each of them personally. The world's leaders were impressed with the new American president.

President Kennedy had been young, handsome, and

suave, with his Boston accent and flashing eyes. The new president was a gangly Texan with huge ears and a twang in his accent. He was virtually unknown by many Americans. But he had been in Washington for over a quarter of a century, and he knew what to do. He had to connect to the stunned Congress and, more importantly, the citizens.

Johnson agreed to speak to a joint session of Congress. He stood at the lectern, a tall, fatherly figure, and began speaking in a soft, subdued voice. He talked about Kennedy's dreams for the country and encouraged, "let us continue." He urged Congress to honor the fallen president and pass a civil rights law that would eliminate from the nation every trace of discrimination. He ended the speech with the familiar words, "America, America, God shed his grace on thee, and crown they good with brotherhood from sea to shining sea." The gathered assembly rose in ovation. Johnson had sounded like a president. America seemed to be in good hands.

Johnson set to work to gather the nation's leaders into his fold. The telephone became "an instrument of national policy." He called businessmen, labor leaders, church people, ethnic groups—hundreds of groups in all. "I need you," he told them. Unlike Kennedy, Johnson knew how to work with Congress to get bills passed. One of Johnson's favorite sayings was, "There are two kinds of horses; there are show horses and there are workhorses." Johnson was a workhorse—he had always considered Kennedy to be a show horse.

Johnson also made a difference in the domestic White House. The Kennedys had projected European elegance, but the Johnsons made it more like an American "mom and pop store" that was open to everyone.

In January 1964, in his first State of the Union message, President Johnson called for a "War on Poverty," a major health program, an effective foreign aid program, construction of homes, schools, libraries, hospitals—and an $11 billion dollar tax cut. By the end of February, he signed the tax cut into law.

Johnson also pushed on the civil rights struggle. His intensity and focus on this issue shocked many, especially the segregationists in Congress, who thought Johnson would not carry through on the bill that Kennedy had introduced. Instead, Johnson told his staff, "I'm going to be the President who finishes what Lincoln began."

In February, the House of Representatives passed a bill that would, unlike earlier legislation, end legal segregation. In the Senate, the bill faced stiff resistance from powerful southern senators. Johnson decided to take his fight to the people and began a series of public speeches advocating its passage. In the speeches, he continuously made reference to the recent murder and kidnappings of African Americans and civil rights workers in the South. He was also able to effectively use the pressure that was being applied by Martin Luther King Jr. and other leaders to convince senators that the time for action on racial equality had arrived.

As they had in the past, southern senators attempted

to filibuster the bill. Previously, they had held the floor until the civil rights bill was removed. This time Johnson said: "They can filibuster until hell freezes over. I'm not going to put anything on this floor until this bill is done."

The Senate debated the bill for five months. Leading the filibuster was Johnson's colleague Senator Richard Russell from Georgia. It took a two-thirds vote to end the debate and, finally, on June 10, 1964, the Senate ended the filibuster, freeing the bill for votes. On July 2, President Johnson signed into law the strongest civil rights bill in the nation's history. The act prohibited discrimination in restaurants, motels, hotels, and places of amusement, libraries, parks, playgrounds, and swimming pools. Schools were to be desegregated. The law withheld federal funds from places that discriminated against citizens based on race, religion, or gender.

President Johnson told the graduating seniors at the University of Michigan in 1964, "we have the opportunity to move not only toward the rich society and the powerful society, but upward to the Great Society." He said that his War on Poverty was priority. Johnson knew what it meant to be poor. He said that it was intolerable that the United States let any child go to bed hungry. He insisted that he wanted to give "a hand up, not a handout" by teaching people new job skills and how to live healthier lives. He began pushing for passage of laws that extended public economic assistance to more poor people.

Johnson traveled the country advocating the pro-

Passage of the Civil Rights Act of 1964 was a significant victory in the fight against legal racial discrimination. *(Lyndon Baines Johnson Library)*

grams that would create the Great Society. Although the Secret Service feared more assassination attempts and pleaded with him to be more careful, he plunged into crowds, shaking hands, beaming, and kissing babies while his guards watched in despair. He sent Lady Bird on publicity trips, including a trip to the played-out mine region of Pennsylvania and to Appalachia.

These efforts paid off with the successful passing of legislation. In August 1964, Johnson signed the Economic Opportunity Act. It established a job corps for training young people, a work-study program to help students in high school and college, provided for basic literacy education, vocational training for mothers and fathers, and established a program of national volunteers called Volunteers in Service for America (VISTA).

Johnson's dream of a Great Society was off to a good start. His record of success getting his plans through Congress was astonishing. He had inherited another issue from the Kennedy Administration, however, that was not turning out as well. In the beginning, there was broad public support for helping the South Vietnamese fight Communist North Vietnam. It was believed that if one country fell to communism, it would make it easier for others to follow. But, in the summer of 1964, two-thirds of the people in the United States thought little of what was happening in Southeast Asia.

Then, in August, just as the Great Society was being implemented, three North Vietnamese torpedo boats attacked the *USS Maddox* in the Tonkin Gulf, which was in international waters, collecting data. The *Maddox* fired back and an American carrier came to its aid. Johnson ordered an American air strike in retaliation, but assured the people this was a "limited response." The United States wanted peace, not war, he said.

He asked Congress to pass a resolution that would allow him to protect American troops in South Vietnam. The so-called Tonkin Gulf Resolution, which passed with only two dissenting votes, authorized "the President as Commander in Chief to take all necessary measures to repel any armed attack against forces of the United States and to prevent further aggression." Johnson interpreted this to mean he was free to fight the war in Vietnam with congressional oversight.

Johnson selected Senator Hubert Humphrey as his running mate in the 1964 presidential election. *(Lyndon Baines Johnson Library)*

As the 1964 election drew near, Johnson left little to chance. He had planned on running as the "peace candidate," but he was now rapidly deploying troops to Vietnam. Republican nominee Barry Goldwater, a senator from Arizona, supported the war in Vietnam. George Wallace and other segregationists, angry with the Civil Rights Act, began an exodus out of the Democratic Party into the Republicans that would eventually result in a historic realignment of political parties.

In August 1964, at Atlantic City, New Jersey, Johnson was nominated by a roaring crowd of Democrats. He gave his acceptance speech on his fifty-sixth birthday, choosing Senator Hubert Humphrey as his running mate.

During the race, Johnson campaigned for forty-two days and traveled six thousand miles. He would frequently stop the motorcade and tell people, "Come on down. Just bring your kids and dogs." Lady Bird and several wives of leading Democrats made a whistle-stop tour of the South on the *Lady Bird Special.* The American people loved the Johnsons during this race. Johnson had been able to reassure the nation after Kennedy's assassination, and Lady Bird's gentleness touched the hearts of the American public. They believed the "President had his hand on the pulse of America."

On election day, November 2, 1964, Lyndon Johnson received sixty-one percent of the popular vote and the second largest electoral college vote in history. Johnson remarked to an aide that, "for the first time I felt truly loved by the American people." That November, the Johnsons celebrated their thirtieth anniversary.

After the victory celebrations, Johnson told his staff, "Don't stay up late. We're on our way to the Great Society." He had no intention of slowing down. He usually worked two shifts of staff. Rising at six A.M., Johnson would be at the office by seven, work to two P.M., exercise, nap, and shower. He would return to the office at four, starting another day with a second shift staff. He was usually in the Oval Office until twelve, unless he was traveling or entertaining foreign leaders or members of Congress.

Johnson ran through aides rapidly. Not only did he overwork them, he could be a terrible bully, saying hurtful things. But he could also be kind and caring. Hubert Humphrey said, "He could take a bite out of you bigger than a T-bone steak and the very next day he would put his arms around you like a long-lost brother." Johnson was a huge personality with huge moods. It was said he was like the weather: ever-present and always changing.

When Congress returned in 1965, he began pushing them to "get on it right now." He laid out three principal goals: Keep the economy going, open opportunities for all Americans, and improve life for all. He wanted new medical research and improved health care for everyone, regardless of their ability to pay.

Johnson strongly believed education could lift people out of poverty, and often remarked that he had not received sufficient education. On April 11, 1965, with his first schoolteacher, Miss Kathryn Deadrich Loney, beside him in front of the former Junction Elementary School, a half a mile from the Johnson Ranch, he signed the Elementary and Secondary Education Act. The bill provided, for the first time, federal aid to education, with a focus on disadvantaged children.

To help prevent crime, he called for better training for police officers. Lady Bird wanted to beautify America, so he set a course to ensure American children inherited a "green legacy." He proposed a national foundation for the arts. But in the midst of this flurry of work to improve the lives of the American people, the war in Vietnam was heading toward a crisis.

Chapter Eight

A Shift in the Winds

President Johnson believed America had committed itself to establishing a stable government in Vietnam. He originally thought a limited war would end in a stalemate, as had happened in Korea a decade before. This assumption may have been the single biggest mistake he made regarding Vietnam. As the conflict escalated, and it became clear that the Communists had no intention of stopping the fight, three choices presented themselves to him: withdraw; wage a limited military action; or fight an all-out war, which would mean bombing North Vietnam.

In early 1965, Viet Cong guerrillas attacked American troops. Eight Americans were killed and several others wounded. In February of that year, an angry President Johnson ordered American planes to attack North Vietnam. He also launched a longer-term air campaign code-named "Operation Rolling Thunder." He said publicly, on several occasions, that he was convinced that the bombing campaign would weaken the Communist's resolve. But secret recordings that were released years later reveal that he was much more doubtful. "Now we're off to bombing these people," he told Secretary of Defense Robert McNamara. "We're over that hurdle. I don't think anything is going to be as bad as losing, and I don't see any way of winning."

The Johnson tapes were recorded over a White House taping system that most people did not realize existed. Johnson, as did Presidents Kennedy and Nixon, wanted the tapes to provide an accurate historical record of his administration. The taped conversations on Vietnam reveal that, privately, Johnson was much less confident about military victory than he appeared to be in public. He insisted that the Viet Cong had to be stopped, "If you let a bully come in and chase you out of your front yard, tomorrow he'll be on your porch." Yet he seemed to believe that nothing short of the use of nuclear weapons would be enough to win the war.

However confused he may have been about America's role in Vietnam, and the possibility of attaining victory at a price Americans were willing to pay, he continued to speak boldly about winning the war. He encouraged the country to stay strong in what he called "the good fight." This discrepancy between the public and private statements of Johnson and others in his administration was the principal cause of the so-called "credibility gap" that would eventually undermine his presidency.

The military escalation created the first stirring of popular opposition to the war. College students and young faculty members, many of whom were subject to the military draft, viewed the war as a threat to their lives. At the University of Michigan campus in Ann Arbor, where Johnson had first announced the "Great Society" to cheering crowds, a protest against the bombings was staged. At the "teach-in," students and faculty discussed whether the U.S. should be involved in Vietnam. The antiwar movement spread across the country. Students and young people everywhere attended protest teach-ins and marches.

Johnson said they were entitled to free speech, but he was concerned. During the 1950s, when fear of communism was at its zenith, he had seen political careers ruined over accusations of being "soft on communism." President Truman had left office a very unpopular man because many felt he had not been aggressive enough in stopping the Communist takeover of China and in prosecuting the war in Korea. Johnson did not want to be the president who "lost Vietnam." But he could feel the shift in the attitudes among Americans. He wrote in his memoirs that by September 1965, he "began to sense a shift in the winds" away from military aggression to stop communism.

To try to bring the war to an end, Johnson proposed a billion-dollar economic development plan for Southeast Asia, including North Vietnam, hoping the proposal would offer a way to open negotiations with the North Vietnamese. He thought improvements, such as electricity, would be an offer Ho Chi Minh could not reject. But he was wrong. North Vietnam insisted on a

Johnson began taping his White House phone conversations in order to have an accurate record of his presidency. *(Lyndon Baines Johnson Library)*

total victory—the uniting of all Vietnam under Communist North Vietnam's leadership. Johnson could not agree to that.

In America, the continuing war spurred greater protests and anti-war rallies. As the number of American troops grew from forty-six thousand to seventy-five thousand, Johnson's advisors began splitting. Some wanted to get out, others wanted more troops and more bombing. Johnson despaired, then grew increasingly depressed as more and more "boxes" (caskets) of "his boys" came home.

In July 1965, Johnson decided to increase the effort even more. Johnson announced a plan to send in fifty-thousand more fighting men, bringing the total to 125,000. He again stated that he was willing to negotiate with North Vietnam, reiterating that he would not settle for a communist Southeast Asia. It still seemed impossible to most people that the best-armed nation in the world would not soon defeat tiny North Vietnam.

During this time, Martin Luther King Jr. met with President Johnson and told him the government needed to do more to protect the voting rights of African Americans. In spite of the Civil Rights Act, several states were still using literacy tests and poll taxes to turn people away at the polls.

On January 2, 1965, King, who had recently won the Nobel Peace Prize, spoke in Selma, Alabama. He pointed out that only one percent of the black population was registered to vote in Selma. King promised to organize a march of citizens to voter registration sites. He intended to make the federal government aware of the

Civil rights leader Martin Luther King Jr. pushed President Johnson to do more for African Americans. *(Lyndon Baines Johnson Library)*

problem. When four hundred African Americans came to the Selma courthouse to register soon after Dr. King's speech, they were arrested and put in jail.

When voting rights marchers attempted to cross the Edmund Pettus Bridge that spanned the Alabama River in Selma, mounted Alabama State Police turned them back with nightsticks, chains, electric cattle prods, and tear gas. Seventeen marchers were injured. The ruthless show of force by the police was captured on television. A few days later, the Reverend James Reeb, a white marcher from Boston, was severely beaten and died of his injuries.

On March 15, with visions of the bloodshed on the Pettus bridge fresh in the congressmen's minds, President Johnson addressed the Congress. "Should we double our wealth and conquer the stars, and still be unequal to this issue of equal rights for black Americans, then we have failed as a people and as a nation," he said. He urged the passage of a voting rights bill. At the end of his speech he raised his arms and spoke the most famous phrase of the civil rights movement: "We shall overcome." The chamber was stunned into shocked silence by the image of the president of the United States, a "wheeler-dealer" from the state of Texas, ending a speech with the anthem of the civil rights movement.

Shortly after the president's speech, a white mother of five who was a member of the march committee in Selma was shot to death.

Johnson applied the full force of The Treatment on

The riots that erupted in Los Angeles in the summer of 1965 quickly sparked similar turmoil across America. Here, Los Angelos police drag a young black man from the front of a looted store. *(Library of Congress)*

the congressmen and senators, and on August 6, 1965, he was able to sign the Voting Rights Act into law. The bill strengthened the previous laws by giving the federal government the power to directly help African Americans register to vote and to protect them against discrimination at the polls. The only legal criterion for eligibility to vote, outside those laid out in the U.S. Constitution, was that a person be registered at their local Board of Elections. All other restrictions were illegal. In only four years, the number of registered African-American voters went from one million to over three million.

Only five days after the Voting Rights Act was signed, rioting broke out in the Watts neighborhood of South Central Los Angeles after the police tried to arrest a young black driver. This modest neighborhood suffered from looting, burning and violence for six hot summer days. Fourteen thousand National Guardsmen were called in to restore order. Before the riot was over, thirty-four people had died. The Watts riot made it clear that racial discrimination was not only a problem in the South.

President Johnson knew that laws were not enough to solve the problems caused by decades of poor education, job discrimination, and poverty. He sent volunteers to live in the ghettos and find out what was wrong. Their reports came back saying how even the best schools there were mediocre and that apartments in segregated neighborhoods were infested with rats and cockroaches. There were few jobs or other opportunities. Johnson

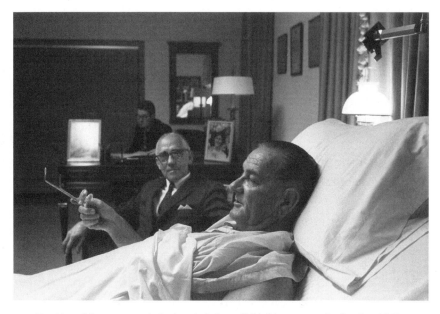

President Johnson entered the hospital for gall bladder surgery in October 1965.
(Lyndon Baines Johnson Library)

read the whole seven-page report aloud to his cabinet. He said he did not want anyone to be ignorant of the poverty in their midst.

Dr. King spoke in Chicago, pleading for decent housing. He tried to teach non-violent resistance, but rioting erupted in Newark, New Jersey, and Detroit, Michigan. The Detroit police and Michigan National Guard could not control the rioting and looting. The governor of Michigan asked the president to send troops. President Johnson sent troops to Detroit, but forbade them to carry loaded guns or bayonets. Still, thirty-seven blacks and three whites died in Detroit, and more than two thousand were injured. Five thousand people were arrested. Damage to homes and businesses from fifteen hundred fires and looting was estimated at $350 million.

Throughout the terrible summer of 1965, Johnson suffered stomach pains. His doctors told him that he needed gall bladder surgery. The operation was a success and soon Johnson was well and "able to make decisions" again. He even showed his foot-long scar to reporters.

The most significant piece of domestic legislation passed in 1965 was the bill that created the Medicare and Medicaid system. For the first time, health care was guaranteed for the elderly and for those too poor to pay. Medicare, along with Social Security, would grow into an integral part of the "social safety net" that Americans have come to rely upon. It would also become the most expensive program in the federal budget.

The Johnson administration had almost unprecedented success in getting its legislation through Congress in 1964. During 1965, the Eighty-ninth Congress passed eighty-nine of the 115 bills Johnson recommended. The bills established the Department of Housing and Urban Development, National Endowments for the Arts and the Humanities, new conservation laws that created and protected federal parks, preserves, historic sites, and seashores. The Highway Beautification Act made it against the law to have billboards and junkyards within a thousand feet of an interstate. This law was a gift to Lady Bird. Johnson often quoted from Rachel Carson's book *Silent Spring*: "No organism before man has deliberately polluted its own environment." A bill to provide college tuition scholarships and low-interest student loans and to establish a National Teacher Corps was passed. This would be the high water mark of the Great Society.

In his State of the Union message of 1966, President Johnson told the country that America was a mighty enough nation to fight the war in Vietnam and still build a Great Society at home. This dual policy was dubbed "guns and butter," and at the time, most Americans approved. His approval rating stood at sixty-nine percent, much higher than Kennedy's before his death. The president was considered the "Most Admired Man" in the world by the 1964, 1965, and 1966 Gallup polls.

Johnson was discovering that his Great Society was hugely expensive and, coupled with the Vietnam War, put immense pressure on the budget. His bills began to meet a less receptive audience in Congress. He had to admit that, "when you're trying to fight in Vietnam and then do everything we need here at home, you've got a problem."

Johnson liked to work in secrecy. Sometimes his strategy was not clear, or he wanted to control who knew his plans. That was how he had worked in the Senate. But instead of saying he did not want to talk about an issue or plan, he would often make up a story. Inevitably, he was sometimes caught in the lies.

His strategy in Vietnam was failing and Johnson did not know what to do. One hundred eighty-five thousand American soldiers were now fighting in Vietnam and 1,350 had already died. The Communists were able to move hundreds of tons of supplies a day into South Vietnam through the jungles on a series of trails and underground tunnels called the Ho Chi Minh Trail.

In spite of all the laws that had been passed and the money spent, poverty, slums, crime, and poor schools remained. Some of the Great Society programs seemed to cause more problems than they answered. In some communities, corruption diverted money into the wrong hands. Critics claimed that the Job Corps provided a place for young inner-city men and women to become involved with revolutionary groups, alcohol, and drugs, rather than learn marketable job skills. Emboldened critics, sensing a shift in public mood, began to call the programs "foolish expenditures" and "training schools for radical strife." Even successful programs such as Head Start, an early education program to help poor pre-schoolers prepare to learn, was attacked.

Johnson negotiated a pause in the bombing in North Vietnam, but the Communists used the time to transport more supplies before breaking the truce. Johnson ordered the bombing to restart. As the war became more unpopular at home, congressmen and senators began to turn against Johnson, who grew increasingly suspicious of even his oldest friends in Congress. Johnson did not want to ask the American public to pay more taxes to support the war, so he did not tell them how much it was costing. At a meeting in Hawaii, Johnson agreed to increase American troops in Vietnam to 430,000.

A three-page advertisement published in the *New*

York Times, signed by more than 6,400 professional men and women, asked the president to "cease all bombing, North and South, and all other offensive military operations immediately." Johnson replied that America must meet its commitment to help South Vietnam and sent American bombers to attack fuel storage depots in the north.

On August 6, 1966, Johnson found joy in the midst of all these problems, when his daughter, Luci Baines Johnson, married Patrick Nugent at Washington's Roman Catholic Shrine of the Immaculate Conception. Seven hundred guests came to the reception at the White House, where an eight-foot high wedding cake was served. Antiwar demonstrators picketed the church and the White House during the wedding.

At the mid-term elections in November 1966, the Democrats lost forty-seven seats in the House of Representatives and three in the Senate. Former Vice President Nixon, who was preparing to run for president in 1968, called the election a "rebuff" of Johnson, whose approval rating dropped to forty-three percent.

Defense spending had climbed to a record seventy-four billion dollars a year. In a speech, Robert Kennedy, who was now a New York senator, criticized the Vietnam War, calling it a human "horror" that must be stopped. Johnson viewed this as a bitter and unfair attack from someone who had been a staunch war "hawk" in the Kennedy White House. Johnson reminded Robert Kennedy and the country that he had stopped the bombing five times, but Ho Chi Minh broke the truce every time. Johnson said in a television interview, "I go to bed every night feeling that I failed that day because I could not end the conflict in Vietnam." The war took its toll as disagreement about what to do continued, and a number of key staff members left Johnson's service.

In January 1967, President Johnson met with other international leaders in the East Room of the White House to sign an international treaty barring nuclear weapons from outer space. It had taken years to negotiate the treaty, and Johnson relished the moment. Just as a toast was being made, a messenger handed him a note. During a test at Cape Kennedy, a fire had broken out in the space capsule and the crew of three was killed. This was a tragic event for the space program.

Martin Luther King Jr. joined in the protest against the war in Vietnam. He argued that the money spent on Vietnam should go to civil rights programs. It was becoming obvious that the country was turning against the war, too. Although polls indicated that the majority of Americans did not think the U.S. should leave Vietnam, protestors heckled and picketed Johnson everywhere he went. Johnson said that the peace movement was undermining the war effort and encouraging the North Vietnamese to continue fighting. By 1967, nine thousand American soldiers had died in Vietnam.

It was not only the antiwar "doves" who turned against Johnson. Soon the hawks, who wanted Johnson to bomb more and wage a full-scale war, were complaining that he was too timid. His approval rating dropped to the lowest point it had ever been.

A "Stop the Draft Week" was organized to begin on Saturday, October 21, 1967. More than fifty thousand protestors rallied at the Lincoln Memorial. The crowd angrily denounced Johnson and chanted, "Hey, hey, LBJ, how many kids did you kill today?" They hurled eggs and bottles, and young men burned their draft cards and left for Canada.

After concluding that the Vietnam War was a lost cause, Secretary of Defense Robert McNamara resigned from Johnson's cabinet. *(Lyndon Baines Johnson Library)*

There was no real front line in the Vietnam War, so it was hard to tell where the war was being fought or if any progress was being made. The Vietnam War was becoming the longest and costliest war ever. Robert McNamara, the president's secretary of defense, admitted privately that he no longer believed the war was winnable. He resigned from the cabinet.

In the midst of all of these problems, President Johnson's first grandson, Patrick Lyndon Nugent, was born. As the months passed and the pressure on him grew, Johnson took solace in watching the baby crawl around his office. In December 1967, his older daughter, Lynda Bird Johnson, married Charles Robb in a wedding held at the White House.

Although his popularity was waning, Congress passed forty-eight percent of the bills Johnson proposed. He signed bills creating the federal food stamp program, the Air Quality Act, a National Commission on Product Safety (that included tamper proof medicine bottle caps and flame retardant children's clothing), the Wholesome Meat Act of 1967, and aid to elementary and secondary education.

At the beginning of 1968, most Americans believed Johnson would run for reelection. For the second time, *Time* magazine named him "Man of the Year." But the war in Vietnam and other domestic problems were taking a cruel toll on him. Lynda's new husband was going to be sent to Vietnam. The deficit in the federal budget had grown to twenty-eight billion dollars, the largest ever. And, although she kept her feelings private, Lady Bird did not want him to run again. She feared he would not live long enough to complete another term.

That year, the president had to take some of the money for his beloved Great Society programs out of the budget in order to fund the war. In four years, the cost of the programs had grown from $6.9 billion to $29.8 billion. At the same time, Vietnam spending had grown to $26.3 billion.

Then, in January, the so-called "Tet Offensive" shocked the country. In Vietnamese tradition, Tet is the biggest holiday of the year, with celebrations that last a week. In the years before, the United States and North Vietnam had always agreed on a truce during Tet. But at midnight on January 30, 1968, seventy thousand Viet

Cong and North Vietnamese made a simultaneous attack on five of South Vietnam's major cities, thirty-four provincial capitals, and sixty-four district capitals. In Saigon, the capital city of South Vietnam, they temporarily captured the presidential palace, the airport, and the headquarters of South Vietnam's general staff. Most critically to U.S. public opinion, they attacked the American Embassy.

The attacks were driven back, and the Tet Offensive was a military failure for the Communists. But psychologically, it was a blow to the American war effort. The Viet Cong suffered much greater losses than the Americans or South Vietnamese, although the South Vietnamese people showed no sign of rising up to fight the Communists, as many war critics had suggested would happen. Johnson at first saw the repulsing of the Viet Cong and North Vietnamese as a victory and ordered 10,500 more troops to be sent to Vietnam, plus more air attacks, to take advantage of the military victory.

In reality, the Tet Offensive marked the beginning of the end of the U.S. involvement in the war. American televisions had been filled with images of gun fights within the walls of the American Embassy and on the streets of Saigon. The military leaders in the war, and the Johnson Administration, had been saying that the communists were almost defeated and the war would be over soon. If that were so, why was there fighting in the streets of Saigon? Although they had lost the battle during Tet, the North Vietnamese and their Viet Cong allies had succeeded in undercutting the remaining support of the war in the U.S. The reinforcements he ordered right after the attack was Johnson's last escalation of the war. It would take another five years, however, before the last American soldier returned home.

Vietnam was the first "television war," and night after night the American people watched films of Vietnamese running from bombings and attacks, jungles and villages bursting into flames. President Johnson watched the war on television, too. He had three sets in his bedroom so he could watch all of the major news reports at the same time.

The deaths and his inability to bring the war to an end haunted him. He had never slept more than six hours a night, but now he prowled the rooms of the darkened White House with a flashlight all night. He became irritable and highly sensitive to any criticism. He seemed to have aged twenty years overnight. He revealed his despair when he privately told a reporter, "I don't know how in the hell to get out."

Chapter Nine

Nobly Done

The first presidential primary is traditionally held in New Hampshire. It is the first critical test of a candidate's strength. In 1968, the only Democratic candidate listed on the New Hampshire ballot was Senator Eugene McCarthy of Minnesota, who was opposed to the war and was supported by cadres of college students. People who wanted to vote for President Johnson had to write in his name. Nevertheless, he won by a slight margin.

After the primary, Robert Kennedy, who sensed after McCarthy's strong showing that Johnson was vulnerable, announced his candidacy. He promised to "end the bloodshed in Vietnam and in our cities." Kennedy's move confirmed Johnson's dislike of him. He thought he was dishonest and could not understand how someone who had been such a hawk during the height of the Vietnam War could now become the "peace candidate."

It looked as though the Democratic Party was going

to be ripped apart in a bruising fight. That he was being challenged by two senators from his own party further indicated Johnson's weakness. His poll numbers had continued to fall, indicating that the majority of voters had lost confidence in his ability to bring the war in Vietnam to an end.

Although there was speculation he would not run, few experienced political observers expected the legendary Lyndon Johnson to leave without a fight. Then, on March 31, 1968, a Sunday evening, Johnson gave a televised speech from the Oval Office in the White House announcing a new Vietnam policy. During the speech the president looked exhausted. His sunken eyes were underlined with dark circles, and his once vibrant voice was weak. This was a far different president than the one who had fought for civil rights and his War on Poverty.

During the address, President Johnson announced that the bombing in most of North Vietnam would cease immediately. He promised that the United States would send representatives to any peace conference if they would be met with good faith representatives of North Vietnam. He said South Vietnam would soon be taking greater charge of its own defense. Still, he said, he would need to send 13,500 more "support troops" to Vietnam in the meantime.

As he was making his speech, his hands trembled and some in the office off camera saw tears in his eyes. Then, as his address drew to a close, his voice grew softer and he calmly said:

Fifty-two months and ten days ago, in a moment of tragedy and trauma, the duties of this office fell upon me . . . With America's sons in the fields faraway, with America's future under challenge right here at home, with our hopes and the world's hopes for peace in the balance every day, I do not believe that I should devote an hour or a day of my time to my personal partisan causes . . . Accordingly, I shall not seek, and I will not accept, the nomination of my Party for another term as your President.

When the speech was over, Lady Bird said, "Nobly done, darling." Lynda and Luci cried. Forty-nine thousand telegrams and thirty thousand letters, most praising him for the dignity of his speech, flooded the White House. The *Washington Post* editorialized that "he has made a personal sacrifice in the name of national unity that entitles him to a very special place in the annals of American history." After the speech, his approval rating jumped to fifty-seven percent.

The day after his withdrawal, Johnson said he felt a great relief. He was looking forward to retirement and maybe a return to teaching. He wanted to watch the bluebonnets bloom in the spring on his ranch. But he still had ten months left to serve as president, a point that was emphasized when, a few days later, North Vietnam said it was ready to open peace talks.

Johnson's own feelings of relief were marred when, on April 4, one of his staff handed him a note that said, "Mr. President, Martin Luther King has been shot." King had turned against Johnson over the war, but

Johnson felt his loss deeply. He pleaded with black leaders to stay calm. He proclaimed a national day of mourning and called on whites and blacks to work together so that Martin Luther King Jr.'s dream would not die with him.

Nothing, however, could contain the rage that swept over the country. Rioting spread through two hundred cities. In Washington, D.C., when black militants threatened to burn neighborhoods, Johnson had to mobilize federal troops to provide protection. Soldiers were stationed around the walls of the White House. On April 10, Congress finally sent a fair housing bill for Johnson to sign. It made it illegal to discriminate against a person renting or buying a residence because of race. Johnson dedicated the law to Dr. King.

Vice President Hubert Humphrey joined Eugene McCarthy and Bobby Kennedy in the race for the Democratic presidential nomination. On June 5, Kennedy was celebrating after winning the California primary. It looked as though he had a lock on the nomination. After giving a short speech to his supporters at the Ambassador Hotel in Los Angeles, television cameras followed him through the cheering crowd down a hallway and into the hotel kitchen. Then a sharp, light crack of gunfire rang out. Kennedy fell to the floor. A pool of blood grew under his head as the American people watched on television. Robert Kennedy had been assassinated.

Although he was no friend of Kennedy, his reaction was heartfelt: "Oh, my God. Not again." It was "too

Robert Kennedy's assassination in June 1968 occurred only two months after Martin Luther King Jr. was shot in Memphis. *(Lyndon Baines Johnson Library)*

horrible for words," he said later. Later, he spoke on television and said, "Americans must stop the violence." Twelve hours later, Congress passed the crime bill Johnson had been wanting. It barred the shipment across state lines and the out-of-state purchase of handguns.

The 1968 Democratic Convention in Chicago was planned to celebrate Johnson's sixtieth birthday, highlight his accomplishments, and pass the torch on to Vice President Hubert Humphrey, who was to be nominated as the party's presidential candidate. Trouble was expected from peace activists, radicals, and militants. Mayor Daley of Chicago was expected to control the protestors. Daley called to duty 11,900 Chicago policeman plus hundreds of plainclothes detectives. Fifteen thousand Illinois National Guardsmen and army troops were held ready. As the convention began, activists clashed with policemen in riot gear. In what many saw as an extreme overreaction on the part of Daley and the Chicago police, tear gas was fired into the protestors, hundreds were clubbed to the ground, and thousands arrested. Newspaper and television reporters were trapped in the midst of swinging clubs and tear gas while reporting the story to a nation that was growing weary of the year of shocking violence.

Inside the convention, arguments between hawks and doves broke out. Many delegates blamed the news media for turning the country against Johnson and the war, and several reporters, including Dan Rather of CBS News, were pushed and shoved by angry delegates and security guards.

Johnson chose not to attend the convention so as not to take attention away from the nominee. He was at his ranch watching the convention on television. Instead of watching the planned celebration of his presidency, he saw himself being pilloried as a villain. An "unbirthday party" was even held where he was denounced and ridiculed. Protestors called him a war criminal and said he was no better than Adolf Hitler. Johnson could not understand how people could feel this way about him.

At last inside the convention hall, Hubert Humphrey was formally nominated as Democratic presidential candidate. Humphrey called the Chicago convention a "catastrophe." At the Republican Convention, the Republicans calmly nominated Richard Nixon, former vice president under President Eisenhower and the man who John Kennedy had barely beaten in 1960, as their candidate for president.

After the Democratic Convention, the South Vietnamese backed out of the Paris peace talks. They feared the peace movement was going to force American leaders to drop them. On October 31, 1968, in an effort to help Humphrey's presidential campaign, Johnson called for a complete halt to all American bombardment of North Vietnam. But nothing Johnson could do would help the Democrats that year. They had to shoulder the responsibility for the war in Vietnam and for the violence in the cities.

Johnson and Lady Bird voted for Hubert Humphrey, but on November 5, 1968, Nixon was elected president in a close election. Johnson tried not to let his disappointment show. He assured the American people that he was still in charge until January 20. In December, the *Apollo 8* orbited the moon ten times, and a beaming Johnson awarded gold medals to the astronauts, Frank Borman, James Lovell Jr., and William Anders when they safely returned. The astronauts gave him a "picture of the ranch" taken from outer space. As his last act as president, Johnson signed an executive order that added more than 7.5 million acres of federally owned lands to the National Park system. Personally, though, the brightest spot of 1968 for Johnson was the birth of his first granddaughter, Lucinda Desha, daughter of Lynda and Chuck Robb.

On the cold, windy inaugural day, January 20, 1969, "Hail to the Chief" played for the last time for President Johnson. Then the band played "The Yellow Rose of Texas." He sat down and Richard Nixon took the oath of office to become the thirty-seventh president of the United States.

As Johnson left office to take up his private life, he was one of the most reviled presidents in history. He had tried to be a man of consensus and to lead the country in a direction that he thought would make a better future. Instead, he left behind a country more divided than at any time since the Civil War. He could not travel around the country without being heckled and shouted at by protesters. He called the day he left office "the happiest day of my life."

He was a sixty-year-old man, in relatively good health, with lots of energy. What would he do? He did

In retirement, Johnson spent time at his ranch with his grandchildren (Patrick Lyndon Nugent is pictured here) and his dog Yuki. *(Lyndon Baines Johnson Library)*

not want to follow President Truman's example and settle into a retirement of reading books. He did not have a hobby. He had lots of money—millions—so there was no reason to go to work.

He decided to work on five major projects: to build the Lyndon B. Johnson School of Public Affairs at the University of Texas, to build the Lyndon Baines Johnson Presidential Library, to see that Lady Bird's memoirs were completed, to write his own book, and to give a series of interviews to Walter Cronkite at CBS News.

Even in retirement, he kept up his work habits. His days began at six o'clock in the morning, when he started barking orders to the ranch foremen and farm crews, demanding reports on how many eggs were laid, how much fertilizer was used and how it was mixed, and if the tractors were working properly. He named his cattle and horses and called them his friends. He knew the families of his workers and the townspeople.

He paid visits to young students and lectured at the University of Texas. He swam often in his pool. He rode his horses, enjoying the Texas land he loved.

Still, there were some reminders of the presidency present. The Secret Service guarded him around the clock. President Nixon sent a courier each week with intelligence summaries. He got frequent telephone calls from Nixon and his staff. Intelligence and military officials visited the ranch for briefings. Old friends visited the ranch and were taken on the inevitable grand tour, speeding for over an hour over dirt roads in his big car. He received thousands of letters a day.

He had several offices in Austin, including one at the Federal Office Building, one at the University of Texas, and one at the Lyndon Baines Johnson Library. The library, built to house all of his thirty-one million papers, was the biggest, most expensive presidential library ever built. Standing eight storeys tall, it had a helicopter landing pad on the roof. Because he felt misunderstood, unappreciated, and disliked by many of his countrymen, the library was Johnson's way of justifying himself. "I want it all there with the bark off," he said, "what I did right and what I did wrong." Even at the library's dedication, protestors showed up to taunt him.

He wrote an autobiography, *The Vantage Point,* but it was criticized and did not sell well. Critics called it "sappy," lacking the Johnson bite. He returned to some bad habits. Although his doctors warned him not to, Johnson began smoking again. His health began to slip. He suffered chest pains and was hospitalized. On his first visit back to Washington, D.C., in April 1970, reporters said he looked "tired, withdrawn."

In April 1972, Johnson suffered a heart attack while visiting his daughter Lynda in Virginia. The doctors said it was so massive that his heart was too damaged for surgery to help. He was dying and he knew it. After five days in the hospital, he went home to the ranch. The doctors ordered him not to smoke, but he went on smoking anyway. "When I go, I want to go fast," he said.

On December 12, 1972, he gathered the civil rights leaders from across the nation at his library and opened his presidential papers relating to civil rights. Even though his doctors told him not to make a speech, he did anyway. In the middle of his speech, he slipped a nitroglycerin tablet into his mouth to ease his chest pains. He said: "We have proved that great progress is possible. And if our efforts continue, and if our will is strong, and if our hearts are right, and if courage remains our constant companion, then, my fellow Americans, I am confident we shall overcome." This was to be Johnson's last speech.

When President Nixon, who was reelected in 1972, took his oath for the second time in January 1973, Johnson could not attend. Two days later, on January

22, he said he was feeling fine, so Lady Bird left for her office in the library at Austin that morning. After lunch, Johnson had an aide drive him around the ranch to inspect fencing. After lunch, he took a nap. Later that afternoon, Johnson called on the phone and asked that the head of his Secret Service staff come to his bedroom right away.

The Secret Service men rushed to his bedroom and found him lying on the floor by his bed. He was dark blue. One agent gave him mouth-to-mouth resuscitation, another called the doctor. They rushed him to Brooke Army Hospital in his private plane, but Johnson died en route. Ironically, that same day a cease-fire agreement was announced in Vietnam.

President Johnson's body lay in state at the Capitol rotunda for seventeen hours while people from all walks of life paid their last respects. He had been a man larger than life, one of the country's greatest legislators, who had risen to the highest office of the land. His work to fight poverty and discrimination was deeply rooted in his memories of being poor, both in his own life and his students', and it was evidence of his deep humanity. His efforts for civil rights helped to finally heal an ugly scar on American life. Despite his personal and political failures, Lyndon Johnson had tried to live up to his father's advice to work for the good of others. At his funeral a reporter said, "No man could have tried harder."

Lyndon Baines Johnson was buried in the shade of a grove of oaks close to the Pedernales River, near his grandmother and Grandpa Sam, and his parents, Sam and Rebekah.

Timeline

1908—Lyndon Baines Johnson born on August 27 in
      Stonewall, Texas.

1912—At age four, Lyndon begins attending Junction School.

1924—Graduates from Johnson City High School.

1927—Enrolls at Southwest Texas State Teachers College.

1928—Attends Democratic Convention as the *College Star*
      editor. Works as a teacher in Cotulla, Texas.

1930—Graduates from Southwest Texas State Teachers
      College. Takes teaching job at Sam Houston High.

1931—Goes to Washington, D.C., as secretary to Congressman
      Richard Kleberg.

1934—Marries Claudia Alta Taylor, "Lady Bird," on
      November 17.

1935—Appointed as Texas Director of the National Youth
      Administration (NYA).

1937—Wins the Tenth Congressional District of Texas.

1938—Reelected to a full term in the Seventy-sixth Congress
      and to each succeeding Congress until 1948.

1941—Loses senatorial race but retains congressional seat.
      Becomes the first member of Congress to volunteer for
      active duty in the armed forces on December 9.

1942—Receives the Silver Star from General Douglas
      MacArthur. Leaves active duty.

1944—March 19, birth of first daughter, Lynda Bird.

1947—July 2, birth of second daughter, Luci Baines.

1948—Elected to the U.S. Senate.

1951—Elected majority whip of the Senate. Becomes chairman of the Preparedness Investigating Subcommittee of the Senate Armed Services Committee during the Korean War.

1954—Reelected to the Senate for a second term.

1955—Elected majority leader of the Senate. Suffers severe heart attack.

1956—Nominated for president at the Democratic National Convention.

1957—Civil Rights Act of 1957 passes.

1958—Guides first space legislation, National Aeronautics and Space Act, to passage.

1960—Elected vice president.

1961—As vice president, serves as a member of the cabinet and the National Security Council, chairman of the National Aeronautics and Space Council, chairman of the President's Committee on Equal Employment Opportunity, and chairman of the Peace Corps Advisory Council. Travels extensively. Advises President Kennedy that a manned moon trip is possible.

1963—After the assassination of President John F. Kennedy, becomes the thirty-sixth president.

1964—Gives "Great Society" speech. Signs Civil Rights Act of 1964. Orders retaliatory air strikes after North Vietnamese attack *USS Maddox*. Elected president.

1965—Great Society programs become the agenda for Congress. Enlarges U.S. commitment in Vietnam. Signs the Voting Rights Act.

1968—Announces he will not run for presidential reelection.

1969—Returns to LBJ Ranch in Texas.

1971—Dedication of Lyndon Baines Johnson Library.

1973—Dies at his ranch on January 22. Buried near his parents and grandparents near the Pedernales River in Texas.

Sources

CHAPTER ONE: A Senator Is Born

p. 9, "A United States Senator . . ." Robert A. Caro, *The Years of Lyndon Johnson: The Path to Power* (New York: Random House, 1981), 3.

p. 9, "He has the Bunton . . ." Ibid., 3.

p. 10, "Would you call him . . ." Ibid., 66.

p. 12, "Whatever they were doing . . ." Ibid., 70.

p. 15, "If you can't come into . . ." Ibid., 74.

p. 15, "Someday I'm going . . ." Ibid., 100.

p. 18, "That boy is going . . ." Ibid., 130.

p. 18, "I'm ready to work . . ." Irwin Unger and Debi Unger, *LBJ: A Life,* (New York: John Wiley & Sons, Inc., 1999) 20.

CHAPTER TWO: Wonder Kid of Politics

p. 20, "What you accomplish . . ." Richard Harwood and Haynes Johnson, *Lyndon* (New York: Praeger Publishers, 1973), 28.

p. 20, "I was rich . . ." Caro, *Path to Power,* 147.

p. 21, "The way to get ahead . . ." Unger, *A Life,* 23.

p. 23, "Politics is a . . ." Ibid., 30.

p. 24, "By God, I'll . . ." Merle Miller, *Lyndon: An Oral Biography* (New York: G.P. Putnam's Sons, 1980), 37.

p. 24, "a young man . . ." Unger, *A Life*, 33.
p. 25, "Act like you're . . ." Ibid., 33.
p. 25, "this wonder kid . . ." Caro, *Path to Power*, 204.

CHAPTER THREE: Congressional Secretary
p. 28, "I felt I . . ." Caro, *Path to Power*, 223.
p. 30, "This skinny boy . . ." Doris Kearns (Goodwin), *Lyndon Johnson and the American Dream* (New York: St. Martin's Griffin, 1976), 73.
p. 31, "The Chief . . ." Unger, *A Life,* 44.
p. 32, "pretty as a little . . ." Ibid., 46.
p. 33, "You've been bringing . . ." Ibid., 48.
p. 33, "Let's get married . . ." Ibid., 48.
p. 33, "If you wait . . ." Ibid., 49.
p. 37, "When I come back . . ." Caro, *Path to Power*, 340.

CHAPTER FOUR: Pothole Congressman
p. 39, "A Vote for Johnson . . ." Caro, *Path to Power*, 404.
p. 40, "We felt he had . . ." Ibid., 418-19.
p. 41, "Measure each vote . . ." Unger, *A Life*, 66.
p. 42, "When I thought . . ." Kearns, *American Dream*, 91.
p. 45, "He was the first . . ." Unger, *A Life,* 76.
p. 49, "JOHNSON WITH 5152 . . ." Ibid., 102.
p. 50, "I felt terribly . . ." Ibid., 105.
p. 50, "The one thing . . ." Kearns, *American Dream*, 95.

CHAPTER FIVE: The Guy Must Never Sleep
p. 56, "I throw my hat . . ." Unger, *A Life,* 134.
p. 60, "be a United States . . ." Ibid., 131.
p. 61, "No prejudice is . . ." Ibid., 147.
p. 64, "The guy must . . ." Ibid., 162.
p. 66, "I have one yardstick . . ." Harwood, *Lyndon*, 43.
p. 67, "one pro-Western . . ." Unger, *A Life,* 171.
p. 68, "most significant . . ." Ibid., 167.
p. 68, "Mr. Eisenhower is . . ." Ibid., 176.

p. 69, "Timing can make . . ." Kearns, *American Dream*, 115.
p. 73, "Johnson can have . . ." Miller, *Oral Biography*, 216.
p. 74, "The Senate is going . . ." Unger, *A Life,* 233.
p. 75, "it was only a pale . . ." Miller, *Oral Biography*, 229.

CHAPTER SIX: Vice President
p. 77, "never said . . ." Unger, *A Life,* 231.
p. 78, "The next president . . ." Miller, *Oral Biography*, 243.
p. 78, "The vice presidency is a good . . ." Unger, *A Life,* 241.
p. 79, "We must offer . . ." Miller, *Oral Biography,* 251.
p. 81, "Jack Kennedy has asked me . . ." Ibid., 262.
p. 81, "If you will get off . . ." Ibid., 264.
p. 82, "Don't let me speak . . ." Ibid., 268.
p. 82, "If the time has come . . ." Ibid., 271.
p. 85, "We never got a thing . . ." Unger, *A Life,* 257.
p. 86, "Don't get out . . ." Miller, *Oral Biography,* 281.
p. 86, "When I looked in the eyes . . ." Ibid., 282.
p. 86, "If Lyndon forgets . . ." Ibid., 281.
p. 86, "Now you-all come to see . . ." Ibid.
p. 90, "Oh, my God, they . . ." Unger, *A Life,* 277.

CHAPTER SEVEN: The President's Hand
p. 91, "This is a sad time . . ." Ibid., 289.
p. 94, "let us continue . . ." Ibid., 293.
p. 94, "I need you . . ." Miller, *Oral Biography,* 341.
p. 94, "There are two kinds . . ." Ibid., 344.
p. 95, "I'm going to be the President . . ." Robert Dallek, *Flawed Giant: Lyndon Johnson and His Times, 1961-1973* (New York: Oxford Univ. Press, 1998), 112.
p. 96, "They can filibuster until . . ." Ibid., 117.
p. 96, "we have the opportunity . . ." Unger, *A Life,* 317.
p. 98, "the President as Commander in Chief . . ." Ibid., 322.
p. 100, "Come on down . . ." Ibid., 328.
p. 100, "President had his hand . . ." Unger, *A Life,* 338.
p. 100, "for the first time . . ." Ibid., 333.

p. 100, "Don't stay up . . ." Miller, *Oral Biography,* 407.
p. 101, "He could take a bite . . ." Unger, *A Life,* 536.

CHAPTER EIGHT: A Shift in the Winds
p. 103, "Now we're off to bombing . . ." *Newsweek.* November
    12, 2001, 59.
p. 103, "If you let a bully . . ." Ibid.
p. 104, "began to sense . . ." Unger, *A Life,* 367.
p. 108, "Should we double . . ." Ibid., 357.
p. 108, "We shall . . ." Ibid., 358.
p. 113, "when you're trying . . ." Miller, *Oral Biography,* 455.
p. 115, "cease all bombing . . ." Unger, *A Life,* 396.
p. 116, "I go to bed . . ." Ibid., 413.
p. 117, "Hey, hey, LBJ . . ." Miller, *Oral Biography*, 488.
p. 120, "I don't know how . . ." Harwood, *Lyndon,* 123.

CHAPTER NINE: Nobly Done
p. 123, "Fifty-two months . . ." Miller, *Oral Biography,* 512-13.
p. 123, "Nobly done . . ." Unger, *A Life,* 460.
p. 123, "he has made a personal . . ." Ibid., 461.
p. 123, "Mr. President, Martin Luther King . . ." Miller, *Oral
    Biography,* 514.
p. 124, "Oh, my God. Not again." Harwood, *Lyndon.*
p. 124, "too horrible . . ." Unger, *A Life*, 468.
p. 126, "Americans must stop . . ." Ibid.
p. 128, "the happiest . . ." Harwood, *Lyndon*, 141.
p. 130, "I want it all . . ." Ibid., 151.
p. 131, "We have proved . . ." Unger, *A Life,* 532.
p. 132, "No man could . . ." Ibid.

Bibliography

Caro, Robert A. *Lyndon Johnson: Means of Ascent.* New
 York: Alfred A. Knopf, 1990.
————. *The Years of Lyndon Johnson: The Path to Power.* New
 York: Random House, 1981.
Dallek, Robert. *Flawed Giant: Lyndon Johnson and His Times
 1961-1973.* New York: Oxford Univ. Press, 1998.
————. *Lone Star Rising: Lyndon Johnson and His
 Times 1906-1960.* New York: Oxford Univ. Press, 1991.
Harwood, Richard and Haynes Johnson. *Lyndon.* A
 Washington Post Book. New York: Praeger Publishers,
 1973.
Kearns (Goodwin), Doris. *Lyndon Johnson and the American
 Dream.* New York: St. Martin's Griffin, 1976.
Miller, Merle. *Lyndon: An Oral Biography.* New York: G.P.
 Putnam's Sons, 1980.
Johnson, Lyndon Baines. *The Vantage Point: Perspectives of
 the Presidency 1963-1969.* New York: Holt, Rinehart &
 Winston, 1971.
Pett, Saul, Sid Moody, Hugh Mulligan, Tom Henshaw, Keith
 Fuller, Supervising Editor. *The Torch Is Passed: The
 Associated Press Story of the Death of a President.* U.S.A.:
 AP Production, 1964.

Unger, Irwin and Debi Unger. *LBJ: A Life*. New York: John
    Wiley & Sons, Inc., 1999.

Websites
President Lyndon Baines Johnson Library & Museum. (official
site) http://www.lbjlib.utexas.edu.

Lyndon B. Johnson. (official White House site)
http://www.whitehouse.gov/history/presidents.

Index